More Tales
Bahamas & Cuba

WM. JOHNSON JR.
Copyright © 2023 William Johnson Jr.
All rights reserved.
ISBN: 9798378615841

Produced by Rachael Miller
Illustrations by Wm Johnson Jr
Cover art by Wm Johnson Jr
Editing by Rob Waldner, Paul Trammell
Layout by Paul Trammell

DEDICATION

This book is dedicated to Rachael M. with Love and to Jim Moody for his friendship.

TABLE OF CONTENTS

ACKNOWLEDGMENTS	5
ODE TO SAILOR JANE	6
FOREWORD	7
CALIPH	9
VALERIE & EUGENE	15
WILLIE & VICTOR	17
WELDER	19
A SCULPTURE COMMISION	22
AN ARTIST & HIS MISTRESS	23
SHARI, PAUL, & MARIE	26
THE LOST YEARS	30
RETURN	32
ABOARD ISLAND GIRL	33
JAMAICA CREEK	37
CAYO VERDE	42
RENATA, THE FIRST MEETING	45
THE MESSAGE	49
ESCAMBRAYS	51
BETRAYAL BY RUDOLFO	53
AFFAIR WITH GUAPITA	55
NOSTALGIA	58
LONG ROAD TO HAVANA	59
LOVERS	61
HAVE YOU EVER	64
TEPOZTECO	65
EL CARISAL	73
DON CARLOS	77
BAHAMA ENTRY	80
EPILOGUE	82
REMEMBER NOW	83
SHORT SNORTER	84
PAUL & THE STRANGER'S SONG	85
THE CONSTRUCTION SHED	88
LOVE POTION	90
FRIEZE AU VENT	92
WRECKS	94
A DRUNKEN SAILOR	95
COOPERJACK CAY	96
ELENA'S TOMB	97
JAPAN JUANITO	98
ED SHEEDY, TOKYO	99
THE HOUSE OF DAWN	100

SANTIAGO	103
FOLDBOATS	104
BOB WHITE IS MISSING	106
THE BERMUDA TRIANGLE	107
EXTINCT THEN FOUND	109
MOND & THE MERMAID	111
BUTTERFLY DREAMS	115
YUCATAN	116
CONCH LIME	119
GORDON SMITH	121
SHERLOCK HACKLEY	124
ON RETIRING FROM THE SEA	125
FLOYD	130
FLOOR SLAB	131
DORIAN	134
AL'S MISTAKE	135
ANN-LOUISE THE LEBANESE	136
ATLANTIC AVENUE	137
ISLAND ARCHITECTURE	138
THE LUCERNE HOTEL	140
BARON ERNEST RITTER Von KREIDNER	142
BLIND CHESS	143
FREDDIE'S WAY	146
FRENCHIE IF	147
JOE COCKER & THE BROWNIES	148
PAIN KILLERS	150
PREGUNTAS	152
SPRING RAIN	153
THE LAST COMMANDO	154
THE TIBURON PENINSULA	155
THERE WAS A WOMAN	156
TRADING SCHOONERS	158
WATER SPOUTS	159
ABOUT THE AUTHOR	161

ACKNOWLEDGMENTS

I wrote More Tales after meeting and getting to know Rachael Miller in the aftermath of Hurricane Dorian. She inspired me to revise old stories and to write new ones. I'm lucky to have such a woman in my life. Without her love and support as well as Rob Waldner's editing, there would be no book.

ODE TO SAILOR JANE

Your sunshine beauty illuminates my soul with songs that only you can sing. Oh Mediterranean Goddess, Botticelli would have painted you as Venus.

FOREWORD

I met Bill during the aftermath of Hurricane Dorian in 2019. I had flown into the Harbour of Elbow Cay on a seaplane in response to the call for nurses and medical relief on the island. It was Jim Moody who took me to check on the folks living in the more remote islands nearby who hadn't yet received medical assessment. This is the day I walked into the life of one of the most captivating and adventurous storytellers I have ever met.

Bill, in his 90's, was articulate, engaging, and seemingly unshaken by the rain, wind, tornados, and Cat 5 hurricane that had skirted his open-air shack and wreaked horror over the Bahamas. He had weathered the storm alone, sturdy, and in true "Bull" fashion.

We bonded straight away and developed a relationship of trust and mutual love for adventure and nostalgia of the times past. He shared with me his paintings and stories of travel and romance. He asked that I help him care for this incredible body of work, to protect the paintings, and see that his final stories made it to print. I encouraged him to recall stories yet untold, and he opened up, from the depths of his memory, and wrote More Tales – fascinating, untold, and always romantic.

Rachael Miller

Rachael "Sailor Jane" Miller and Wm. "Bill" Johnson

CALIPH
A World of His Own

He hardly knew how or why, but Caliph suddenly found himself on his own in a world he knew little about. It didn't bother him very much, because he was only twelve at the time of his orphanage and was fortified with the illusions and vast energy of that age. His skin was piel canela, the colour of stick cinnamon, and his brown hair was cut long and nearly hid his eyes.

Caliph was a bush boy with no formal education. He knew nothing of the world beyond the shores of his small island. However, there was little he did not know about the island on which he lived and the shallow waters around it. He knew where the wild Guinea corn grew in the pine barrens, where there was fresh water in a well, at what phase of the moon to gig lobsters on the grass flats, and where ground doves laid their eggs. Caliph's life was a full and innocent experience within the limits of his island environment.

There were other people on the island, three families in all with ten children among them. After his father died, they helped him bury the old man, but that was all. They felt that Caliph, like his father, was a bit wild and not to be trusted. After all, the father and son lived far down the shore and had little to do with anyone.

After the funeral, Caliph went away. In time he was forgotten. Caliph knew nothing of the prejudices of the people. It was not worth bothering about. He had more immediate things to concern him.

Having no brothers or sisters, Caliph easily accepted the fact that there was no one to play with. His sole companion had been his father, and that was all he needed.

During the year before Old Caliph died, he wasn't much company for his energetic son. Most of the time, he sat on the rocks at the mouth of the creek staring out to sea as though waiting for a sea god to rise up and claim him. Caliph would sit with his father for a while until he became restless. Then he would run down the beach, explore the creek, or walk inland to the pine barrens.

When Caliph was younger, his father went with him everywhere and taught him about plants and animals, the earth and sky, and about their true and imagined relationships. Old Caliph was a simple person, a man of the bush and seashore. Like his son, he had no education, but like many primitives, he possessed a store of local knowledge. Old Caliph loved truth and knowledge. Caliph learned much from him.

When the boy brought him a new plant to identify, Old Caliph would come alert momentarily and tell him if it was edible or if it had medicinal qualities. Then he would lapse back into silence. It all changed when Old Caliph died.

One day, he called his son to him, and laying a hand on the boy's shoulder he said, "I'll be leaving you soon and there is something I want you to find, something I had many years ago." For a moment the old man's eyes glowed with the flame of youth.

"What is it poppa?" Caliph asked.

"It's something that's easy to find," his father said and added, "But it's just as easy to lose."

"What is it Poppa?" Caliph asked with awakened curiosity. "Please tell me."

Old Caliph's lips parted in a toothless smile and he looked lovingly at his son.

"What I want you to find," he said. "Cannot be put into words or drawn in the sand. I had it once. Then I lost it." He hesitated. "You must find it yourself."

Old Caliph paused in thought. "If only your mother…," he said and turned to look at the sea.

"I don't understand, poppa," Caliph said, but his father just smiled and said, "You'll understand when you find it."

Caliph was confused. He understood even less when his father was gone.

After the funeral, Caliph hung around the village for a few days. The people fed him, but when he left, they were relieved.

"Just like his father," they said. "He's wild and independent and he wants to be alone." Then it was as if he did not exist and had never existed.

Caliph went back to the thatched hut his father built, the hut in which he was born, and where his mother died.

Caliph's first night alone was difficult, but at first light, he remembered his father saying, "Dawn is the birth of day." He remembered too, how he welcomed the sun with raised arms. Those memories helped Caliph through the first lonely day he had ever known.

Caliph kept to the family ritual of bathing in the sea each morning. Small fish came to him and he broke open a sea urchin to feed them. Every morning when he washed, the fish were there. After a while he gave them names.

For food, Caliph pried molluscs from the rocks and dug clams on the tidal flats. He set fishing lines in the creek to provide dinner, and every day he worked in the potato patch, weeding and planting. His father had taught him how to alternate plantings so as to have a constant crop, and how to plant the seeri potatoes in mounds. Caliph tended the plants just as his father had and he buried fish bones in the ground to enrich the soil.

"Never waste," Old Caliph told him. "Give back to the earth what you don't use and you'll never go hungry." He was the sort of man who told the why of things. In everything Caliph did, the words of his father came back to him.

The hot, newly-turned soil under his bare feet gave Caliph a feeling he could not put into words. Words in fact, were becoming a part of his past. He did not try to express himself as before. There was no one to talk to. Caliph was alone, but he was not lonely.

Caliph often thought about what his father said before he died, and the same puzzlement came over him. What was it that his father wanted him to find? What was it that he must discover for himself? The more Caliph wondered, the more confused he became.

When the sea was too rough to fish or to dig for clams, Caliph would walk inland across the savannah and into the pine barrens. There, he would weave a palm leaf basket and fill it with spices and herbs. On the way back, Caliph stopped at a stone well to drink and rest in the shade of a fig tree. The well was known as the Pirate Well, and it was so old that not even old Caliph knew its history. When Caliph dipped his coconut shell cup in the well, he filled it and drank only half. He poured the remainder back into the well. It was something his father did. So, out of respect, Caliph followed the ritual.

At the mouth of the well, there were lines carved in the rock. To Caliph they were just a pattern of lines. Yet they fascinated him, and each time he was at the well, he studied them, trying to make out what they represented.

Then, one day, as in a dream, the lines came into focus for him. It was a ship! So crudely rendered and so badly eroded, that he could barely make it out.

Months later, Caliph was at the well, sucking the last drops from a dove egg, when he remembered a skiff his father found on the beach after a storm. They had moved it into the creek and put it bottom up on the bank. The next day, Caliph waded up the creek and found the skiff where they left it, covered with palm fronds to protect it from the weather. The palm fronds had long since rotted and blown away.

Fortunately, it had been left in the shade. Caliph could see it needed a lot of work before it could be launched. He set to work, filling the seams with resin from a gum-elemi tree, mixed with gum from a sapodilla tree.

He worked for three days, caulking and filling the seams, and at night he dreamed of going to sea in the boat.

The seed of adventure had been planted in him as a baby, when his father took him to sea in a boat. He remembered water sounds and rhythmic movement, warm sunlight, and his father's shadow, shielding him from the glare. Caliph longed to experience those feelings again. He wanted to see what lay beyond the horizon and to look back across the water at the land.

Caliph wondered if he would see where the gulls went each morning, or where the frigate bird nested at night. The island Caliph knew so well had become something to go beyond. It took all the skill of leverage he learned from his father for Caliph to launch the skiff. When it was afloat, he picked up a stout pole, waded out, and climbed aboard. With his feet on the boat's planking, it was as if he was standing on water. A familiar feeling came over him.

Caliph poled the skiff down the creek, across the alluvial sand bar, and over the grass flats. An offshore wind carried him over the barrier reef and into the ocean. Caliph stood, looking back at the beach, with his hut and the rocks at the mouth of the creek. The sun shone bright in a cloudless sky. Soon the island was out of sight. A porpoise rolled beside the skiff and a flight of gulls passed overhead. Caliph laughed with joy and raised his arms to the sky. He was in a world of his own making.

The thatched hut blew down in a winter storm, and with no one to tend them, the potatoes grew rampant from mound to mound. The ground doves laid their eggs and proliferated, undisturbed.

If anyone missed Caliph, it would have been the fish he fed each morning. However, after a while they too forgot him.

Before he joined his parents, Caliph found what his father could not put into words or draw in the sand.

It was Happiness!

Originally published as "A World Of His Own" in Skipper Magazine,
Vol. XXVII, No. 7, July 1967.

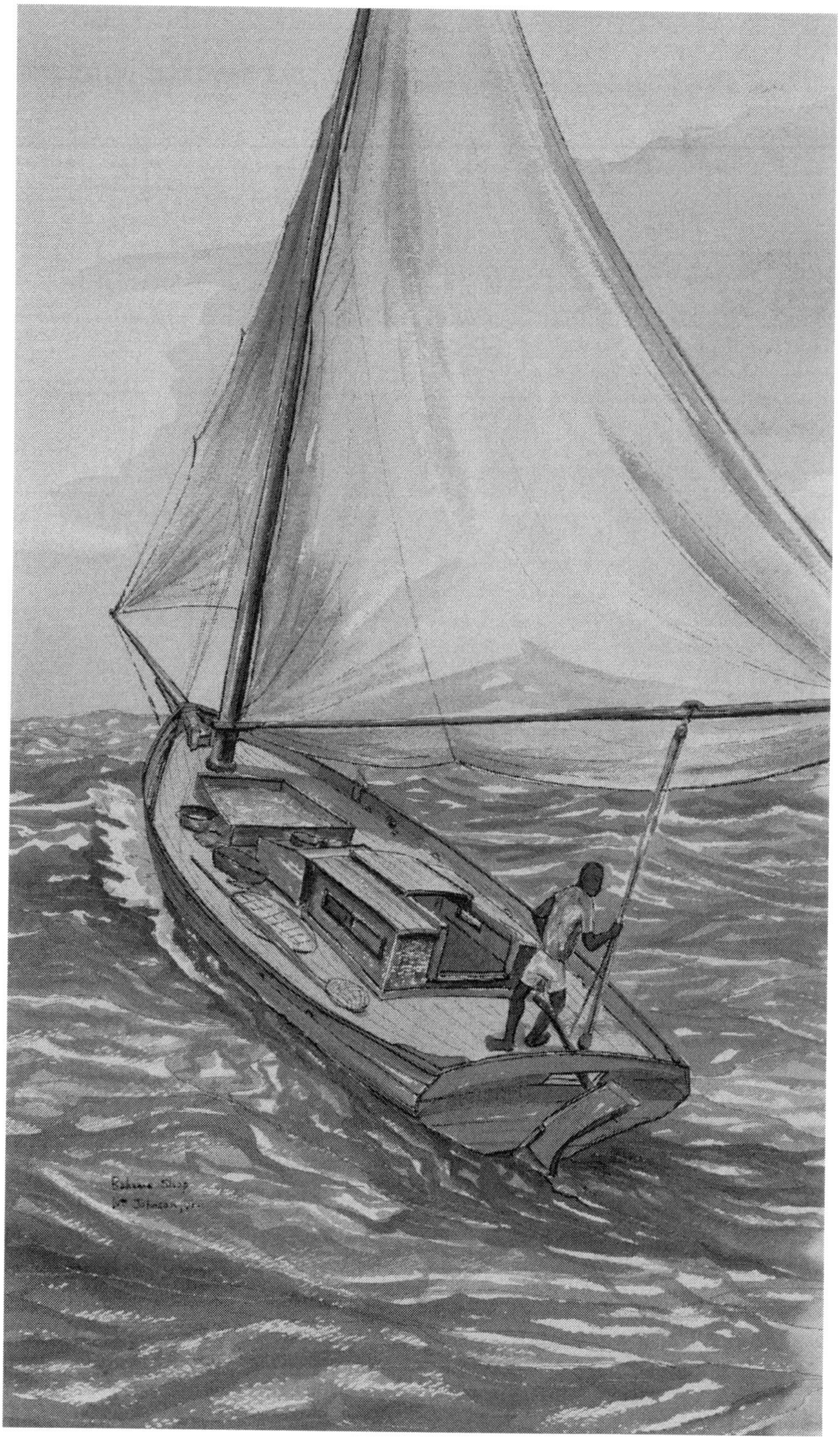

VALERIE & EUGENE

Things must have been tough in 1930, the year before I came into the world, and it became worse in the years ahead. Uncle Marion turned over the Wyeth Building to my mother and father and went north to find work. My parents lived in the top floor apartment. The architects' office was on the second floor. Below the drafting room was an empty apartment. One day, a middle-aged lady came to the door looking for work. When my pregnant mother said there was none, the lady asked for food. It turned out that due to the depression, she and her husband were jobless, broke, and homeless.

My parents fed the couple and moved them into the vacant apartment downstairs.

After I was born, the wife, Valerie, became my nursemaid and babysitter. Her husband, Eugene, found a few odd jobs around town. They were decent people and a great help to my parents. Soon I was living with them downstairs. Valerie and Eugene took care of me for seven years until they got back on their feet and moved away.

One of my first memories is of an inchworm that I named Henry. I found him measuring his way along the branch of a Surinam cherry tree. I kept him in a shoe box. He was my first pet. When I looked in the box one day, Henry was gone and there was something white and fuzzy there. Eugene explained that Henry was still there, but in a cocoon. I didn't understand. All I knew was that my pet was gone. I was upset.

A week later, I opened the shoe box and a butterfly flew out. I was mystified until Eugene explained the wonders of metamorphosis to me. I learned that nothing stays the same, that all things change, and sometimes it's for the best.

Eugene was a kind man. He always took time to explain and show me things. He taught me how to bait a hook, hold the line, and strike when the fish took it. The first fish I ever caught was off the old Palm Beach Pier and it was with Eugene's help. It was a good size sailor's choice. I remember how it flapped silver in the sunlight.

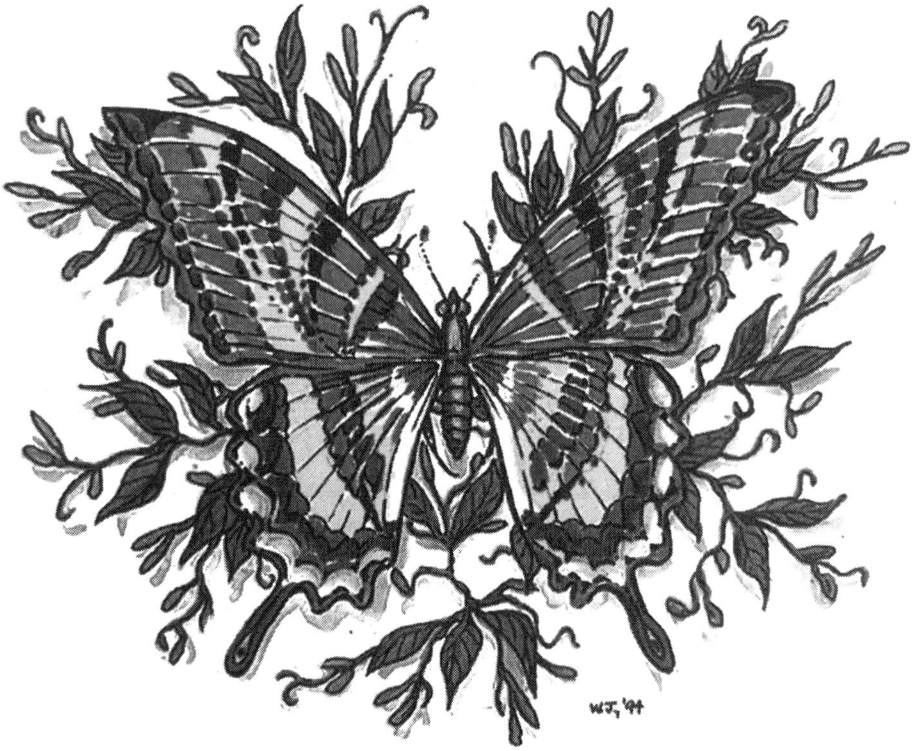

WILLIE & VICTOR

I was born at the height of the Great Depression, and I knew nothing of the hardships my family and others endured. It was not until I was an adult that I met two men who coped with it in a unique way.

Willie Wilson and Victor Brant left their homes in North Dakota and took to the road on bicycles. In those days many men left home and family to wander America and find better lives. They were the hobos, the vagrants of today.

Willie and Victor were no hobos. They were accomplished musicians on their way to find work in Music Land, New Orleans!

Their story starts in North Dakota in the early 1930s. Willie's dad was a carriage painter specializing in lacquer and pin-striping. Willie, while keeping up with his music, apprenticed to his father. He became an expert at striping, gold-leafing and Chinese lacquer. I never knew what Victor did for a living, but I believe it was woodworking.

When the depression grew worse, the two friends took to their bicycles and headed south. They carried only a few essentials: Willie his trumpet and Victor his guitar. They slept in fields and barns at night and travelled south during the day.

After two weeks, they reached New Orleans and landed a gig in a jazz club. Their arrival was well-timed, for it was the Blues Era. They played with music greats like Louis Armstrong and Robert Johnson. Then, when Petrillo formed the Musicians' Union in 1919, Willie and Victor threw down their instruments and never again played in public.

By then, they had saved enough money to buy a 30-foot sailboat, a Tahiti Ketch. Being from landlocked North Dakota, they knew nothing about boats or the sea. Nevertheless, they set sail across the Gulf of Mexico bound for Florida. By the grace of God, they made it to Miami.

While in Miami, Victor met a woman, got married, and moved to New Jersey. There he worked in a shipyard, and in his spare time, he built a sailboat.

Willie remained in Miami, living aboard the Tahiti Ketch and made a living varnishing yachts.

When I first met Willie and Victor, they were doing well. Victor had a large sailboat in which he and his wife cruised to Florida each winter. Willie had sold the Tahiti Ketch and was living in a marina aboard a smaller boat.

Whenever they got together, they played music, Willie on trumpet and Victor on guitar. When I got to know them, they told me about joining the army and serving as military policemen during the North African campaign.

When I last saw Willie and Victor, they were living productive lives and playing the music they loved.

WELDER

One day while visiting Pops at his home in Palm Beach, I bought a welding set on sale at the Sears store. It was complete with gauges, hoses, and a cutting torch. It cost every cent I had. When I showed it to Pops, he bristled.

"What are you going to be," he said derisively, "a Welder?" Pops was still upset about my giving up architecture for marine biology.

I returned to "Island Girl" in Coconut Grove and began a series of welded copper insects: butterflies, beetles, and cockroaches. They were decorative and fairly realistic with bronze and phosphor copper melted on copper plate and corroded with sea water. One rainy night, a friend of mine was startled by one of my copper cockroaches I had left on the dock.

Interior decorators started buying my insects and I began to make a living. I welded a three-foot-long fish skeleton using 16-gauge iron plate, coat hangers and welding rod. I mounted it on grass-cloth and framed it. A decorator saw the fish skeleton, bought it right away, and commissioned me to do another. I was so encouraged that I produced a series of fish skeletons, all of which were purchased by the Knoll Furniture Company in New York.

Over time, my welding technique had improved and I began doing human forms with intricate facial features and other details. My sculptures were exhibited at art shows and displayed in local galleries, and when a picture of a piece appeared in the newspaper, Pops' attitude changed.

A few years later Bill Woods, curator of the Norton Gallery arranged a father-and-son show of Pops' oil paintings and my sculptures. It was a success and most of the pieces sold.

Later in the Bahamas, I did a series of forged and welded iron Wind Witches and one was purchased by Arpad Plesch, the European art dealer. I've been told it's at his estate in France alongside a Giacometti and a Henry Moore. How flattering and again, how encouraging!

When Sir Desmond Cochran commissioned me to do a sculpture for an alcove in his Eleuthera house, I created a rather abstract Bahamian sculler with English copper pennies melted over iron. I corroded it with sea water which gave it a greenish-blue patina. Sir Desmond loved it.

Besides sculpture, I was working nights at a Junkanoo Club and doing exploration surveys for various real estate companies. I formed a limited company named Explorations, Ltd.

Word of my work got around. Robin and Malcolm McAlpine commissioned me to survey Bell Island in the Exumas. When it was done, they looked at the island from the air and on the basis of my survey, they bought it without ever setting foot on it.

That was a turning point in my life as many more jobs came my way. Little San Salvador, Joulters Cay, Fish Pond Eleuthera, Tongue of the Ocean survey for Continental Oil.

Explorations Limited, a one-man company, went into business.

Note: Bell Island has changed hands over the years, and today (2011) it's owned by the Aga Khan III.

Another Encouragement
While working at Junkanoo Club, I met the English interior decorator, Dick Stickney. He commissioned me to do artwork for Club Peace & Plenty in George Town, Exuma. I did fifty small watercolour and pen & ink illustrations of Bahamian sea-life; fish, crabs, shells, etc. Stickney had them matted and framed and he hung them in the guest rooms at Peace & Plenty. I was well paid for my efforts, but within a year, Stickney wanted fifty more and they had to be twice the size of the first ones.

It seems that my small framed pictures fit easily into suitcases and the hotel guests were stealing them. A compliment to my artwork perhaps.

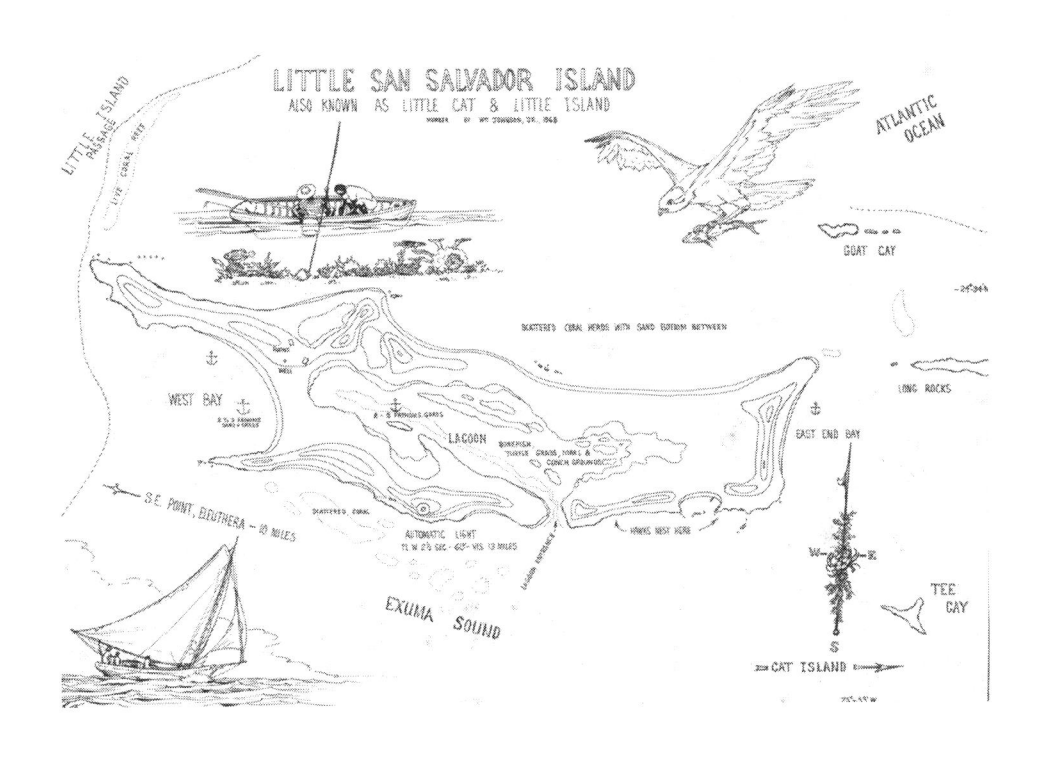

A SCULPTURE COMMISION

Sir Desmond Cochrane commissioned me to do a sculpture for his new house in Eleuthera. The house was designed by Ray Nathaniels, the Nassau architect who reminded me of the gaunt French architect, Le Corbusier.

It was a bold design with cantilevered balconies and many stucco alcoves. There were compound angles to every wall. I completed a welded iron "Sculler" in the style of Giacometti, and Sir Desmond loved it. Nathaniels had designed a niche just for the sculpture, and it stood there casting shadows on the white stucco walls. As a coating for the "Sculler," I melted English copper pennies and phosphor bronze over the black iron form. As time passed, a reddish-green patina grew in the salt air of Eleuthera. Because of that feature, I considered it a "living sculpture."

Sir Desmond, a titled Englishman, was married to a daughter in the Sursock family of Beirut, Lebanon. His in-laws were one of the wealthiest and most influential families in the Middle East. They were so wealthy in fact, that they financed Abdul Nasser's rise to power in Egypt.

During my mother's trips overseas, she often stayed with the Cochranes at Palais Sursock in Beirut. Perhaps my sculpture commission had something to do with her friendship with them. Unfortunately, by the end of the twentieth century Beirut was in turmoil and Palais Sursock was in ruins.

AN ARTIST & HIS MISTRESS

It was 1942 and the war in Europe wasn't going well for the Allies. In Palm Beach, there were air raid wardens (my dad was one) and aircraft and submarine spotters (uncle Marion was a spotter). Oil tankers were being torpedoed offshore and the Coast Guard patrolled our beaches on horseback. An artillery battalion was stationed at the inlet and there was an Army/Air Force base at Morrison Field in West Palm Beach. Things were changing fast.

Unlike the big cities of the eastern seaboard, Palm Beach didn't take well to the refugees flooding America. The only exceptions were some White Russians; elegant gentlemen with continental manners, who fit in well with the snobbish Palm Beach elite. One I remember was Serge "Obie" Obilensky, who made his entrée teaching backgammon (then, an unknown game in America) and as a chess master. The gentry accepted him immediately.

The other refugee I remember was an Italian artist named Ricardo Magni and his American mistress Virginia, who moved into a rundown house on Royal Palm Way. Ricardo was an artist in the classic mold and his specialty was Trompe L'oeil. Before long, he transformed their dilapidated home into a fantasy world of vine-hung lintels and Greek and Roman marble columns with ornate capitals, all rendered in realistic detail. Ricardo painted cracks in the walls, chips on his marble columns, and dried leaves in the crevasses of the acanthus leaves on the Corinthian capitals. Here and there was a lizard or a frog stalking an insect on a Phoenician frieze.

I was eleven when I first entered the fantasy world of Ricardo Mangi's genius and I can picture it even today. The room that impressed me most was the smallest one in the house, the bar.

The first time I saw it, my dad had me close my eyes and he led me in. When he told me to look up, I beheld a clear blue sky with birds wheeling high above. I was seeing it through a gaping hole in the ceiling, or so it seemed. We were standing in a bombed-out ruin of a room with its brick walls blown open, and there was ivy growing over the rubble. There were four destroyed walls and four views aside from the sky overhead. One wall had vines growing over the rubble and a frog facing a lizard. The view behind the bar was of a rolling countryside framed in broken rock. Was it Ricardo's memory of Tuscany?

I looked back at the entrance with its damaged doorway and cracked marble lintel, and then I turned to the east. Framed by a blasted, rubble-strewn wall was a vast empty beach running down to a seaweed-strewn shoreline and a calm blue ocean. There were no sails on the sea as I expected, but there were footprints on the beach leading from the foreground, away to the left and out of sight.

That room was Ricardo's masterpiece. He had transformed and expanded a small dark space into a brilliantly lit, all-encompassing panorama.

Ricardo was ostracized by Palm Beach society because he and Virginia were unmarried. He offered to give painting lessons, but there were few takers. He approached several art galleries hoping for a show of his works, but with no luck. The pariah couple's only friends were my dad and mom, and of course me. My father was an architect and an accomplished artist in his own right. He appreciated Ricardo Magni's unique talent and his intellect. Also, there was a subtle kinship between the men because my mom's name was Virginia.

After two years in Palm Beach, being rejected by the gentry, with little work and no money, Ricardo Magni killed himself.

When I was older, my dad told me how he did it. During an appendix attack, he took a massive dose of laxative.

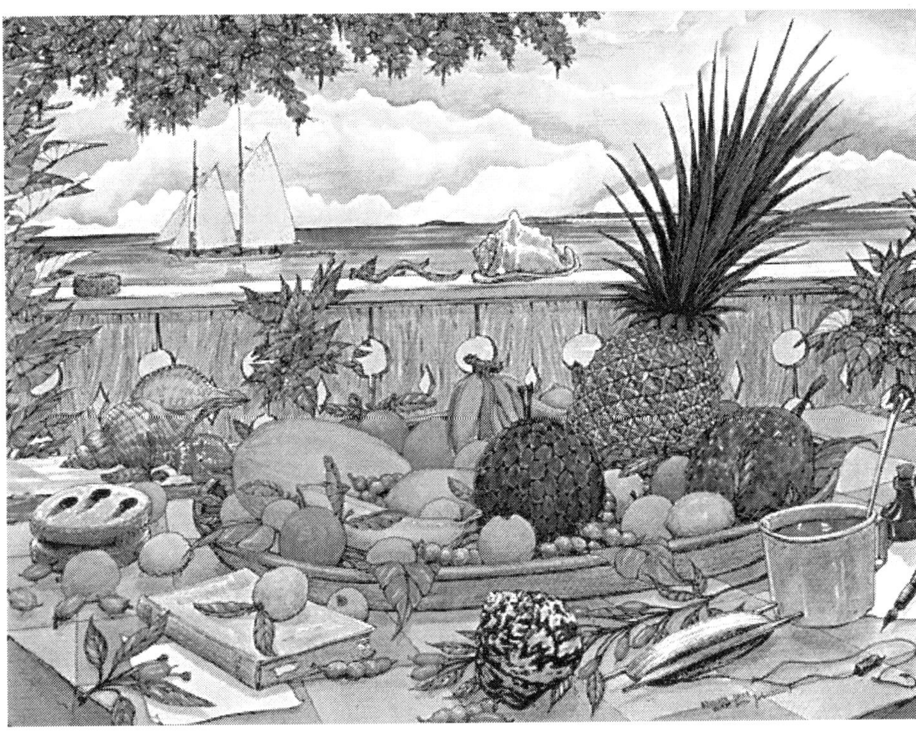

Shari, Paul, & Marie
It is said that love is a sorceress

Shari

Shari was a beautiful, wild-spirited woman from the world of high fashion, a supermodel before the term was used. She graced the covers of Vogue and Bizarre and was photographed by Avedon. Her modelling career began at seventeen, reached great heights, peaked, and rapidly declined. She was married to an older man, an Austrian fashion photographer. They had a son together. Being a realist, Shari stepped aside in deference to younger models and retired gracefully.

I met Shari when I was 22 and she was 35. I was living in a marina aboard my sailboat. She was supervising a fashion shoot nearby. She took an interest in the marble sculpture I was carving. That night during a thunderstorm she returned to my boat, slid open the hatch and crawled into my bunk. She cast a spell over me.

We spent the summer in Key West in a double-gabled house on a side street off Duval. We basked in silver moonlight in the rooftop valley, smoked pot, conversed, and recited poetry. We teased, touched, fondled, and made love under the stars until our bodies seemed as one.

That summer, Shari's worldly experience and intellect inspired me to create some of my best works. Although we were from vastly different worlds, Shari and I were well matched in many ways. I was primitive and she was sophisticated. Ever the romantic, I fell madly in love with her. When she said she cared for me, I took it for love. That was all I needed and love had never tasted so sweet.

In the fall, guilt turned Shari back to New York and to her estranged husband. By winter, she was living a life she had no use for and little interest in; a life that eventually destroyed her.

Paul Chataux

Those months in Key West with the beautiful Shari were idyllic and a welcome change from the islands and the hills of Cuba. One of our friends was Paul Chataux, an elderly Frenchman who, in his youth, had been a long-distance swimmer. Now that he was too old for that, he thought of a scheme to have a shark tow him a long distance. He constructed a harness for a large shark that would tow him from Havana and across the Gulf Stream to Key West. He had a friend in Cuba looking for a suitable shark.

Some years earlier, Paul had attempted the same stunt in Miami by having two bull sharks tow him to Bimini. He got as far as the mouth of the Miami River when one of the sharks bit him. Paul showed us a scrapbook with newspaper accounts of his distance swims and the failed shark-pull to Bimini. Paul was a consummate dreamer and he referred constantly to "Le shark" that would bring him fame and fortune.

He showed us a children's book he wrote and illustrated. Shari wanted to have it published. We visited Paul often at his trailer home where we drank daiquiris in the shade with the shark harness hanging in the tree above.

Marie de Marsan

Another friend was Marie de Marsan, an accomplished artist who lived in squalor amongst tubes of paint, brushes, sketch pads, and her works of art. The house smelled of turpentine and linseed oil.

That summer, Marie did an oil portrait of Shari nude from the waist up, holding a spiny lobster. She must have known I was in love with Shari because she gave me the charcoal sketch for the painting. I never saw the finished painting, but the sketch was pure magic. It was a perfect likeness of Shari in charcoal on tracing paper. It captured her dark eyes, her erotic beauty, and all the doubts and worries that consumed her that summer.

The sketch was destroyed years later during a hurricane in the Ragged Islands. I consider it one of my greatest losses.

The last time I was with Shari before she left for New York, she said, "You know I care for you." Then she added, "But I don't dare love you."

I wondered why…

"Because you would have other women. It's your nature and it would hurt me." Shari knew me too well.

A young love's dreams never come true. I should have known that...

El amor bruja!

Blondie

THE LOST YEARS

Key West was hot that summer, sometimes 92 in the shade, or even 94. A quarter mile from Hemingway's old home on Whitehead Street, I re-read "To Have and Have Not." When I put it back on the shelf, I said to myself, "I had it. I had it all with Shari, all a man could ever want. Now that she's gone, I have Not!"

So I returned to the tropics, to the monkey noise where brown-skin boys and bare-foot girls danced to rada drums, where boats were loading at old stone quays, and trading schooners returned from the lonely seas. I paused for a moment in the banyan shade, stopped and looked about me at the sea of jade, and noticed as I turned how the tall palms swayed, how the drums in me beat as I went on my way.

I went back aboard Island Girl and sailed into the vastness of the southern Bahamas, where I lived in blessed solitude for some time before sailing to Cuba to find Tula.

In the winter, I returned to the Bahamas aboard Island Girl. That spring, sailed to the Magic Island, William Seabrook's Haiti.

But that's another story…

Shari's spell lingered on. I kept a self-serving journal and wrote romantic poetry in English and Creole. I had not yet discovered the beauty of Haikus. Later I consigned it all to the sea.

What brought me back to reality was a brush with death on my last trip to Cuba. It was the second time in my life that the Grim Reaper looked at me with hungry eyes and blinked. My focus was on Tula, on the here-and-now of her presence, and the reality of her Latina beauty. I was loved and still capable of loving. Again, I believed I was with a perfect woman. How naive I was and how foolish!

Note: On Thanksgiving day 1999, Shari was raped and murdered on Staten Island.

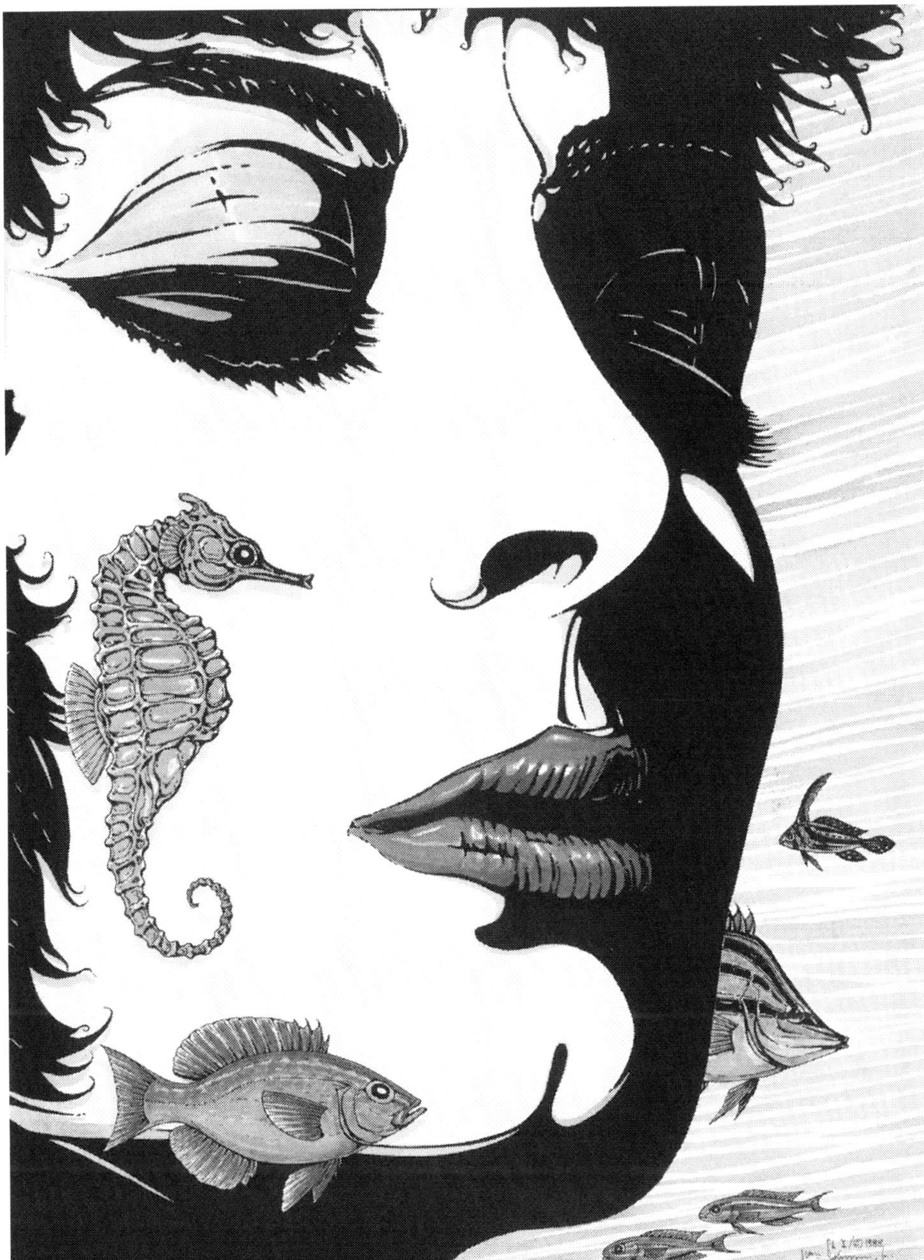

RETURN

Return to the tropics and the monkey noise
Where barefoot girls and brown-skin boys dance to rada drums
Where boats are loading at old stone quays,
Come trading schooners from the lonely seas.

You pause a moment in the banyan shade,
Stop and look about you at the sea of jade,
And notice as you turn
How the tall palms sway,
How the drums in you beat as you go your way.

I remember reading Robert Gibbings' "Over the Reefs and Far Away" the year before. I believe that book, and Kipling's poetry inspired my poem.

ABOARD ISLAND GIRL

Island Girl was a lovely vessel, not a fancy yacht by any means. Her topsides, decks, and cabin were painted white. The only bright work was her varnished tiller, a natural crook of native mahogany. It fit Neil's hand as if it had been made for him. Island Girl's hull was similar to the half-model designs brought to the Bahamas by British Loyalists during the American Revolution.

She was built in 1945 by the Abaco shipwright, William Albury. After the 1949 hurricane, Neil bought her, made repairs, and re-rigged her as a ketch. Island Girl was twenty-five feet from stem to stern, eighteen feet on the keel, and she displaced five tons. Under sail at sea, she was safe, fast, and handled like a vessel twice her size. With her three-and-a-half-foot draft, she was ideal for the shallow Bahamas.

Neil sailed Island Girl for two years without an engine. When he was commissioned to paint a mural and was paid for it, he bought a Lister Diesel engine. When it was installed in his beloved vessel, he was able to venture beyond the Bahamas to Haiti and Cuba. Neil Gardiner loved Island Girl as if she was a woman. With his hand on the tiller, she responded likewise.

It was late afternoon on a hot summer day. Island Girl was anchored in the lee of Potters Cay. Neil and his friend Don were lounging in the shade of the mizzen awning, drinking the traditional farewell libation of the islands, rum and lime juice without ice. Neil was scheduled to leave Nassau the next day for Acklins Island. There, he was going to pick up cargo and transfer it to a vessel at Cayo Verde. As usual, Ruiz had arranged everything.

Neil was squinting down the harbour into the glare where a smack boat was attempting to come about. It had rounded up into the wind and was caught in stays. An elderly black man stood at the tiller shouting orders to a frenzied crew trying to back the jib. The vessel sailed astern until the mainsail finally filled and it fell away on the port tack. As the smack gathered way, the helmsman sat down to fight a weather helm.

Neil turned to Don. "That's old Captain Moss," he said smiling. "Every tack is an adventure for that guy, and when he anchors it's a disaster."

Don laughed. For he too knew Captain Moss. He took a sip of rum and changed the subject. "Tula told me you refused to take her with you to Acklins."

The sun was dropping fast. So, Neil stood and adjusted the awning. "It's a blue water sail and it's too risky!" he said as he tied a rolling hitch on the backstay.

Don watched his friend tie the hitch and he thought, "He takes pleasure in everything he does, from tying a knot to steering a compass course, or painting a picture." Don envied that quality in Neil. "Tula's feelings are hurt," Don said. "She wanted to sail with you."

Neil growled and took a drink. "She'll get over it," he replied.

Don had seen changes in Neil since his return from Mexico. Before Tula came into his life, Neil had gone from one woman to another, fucking indiscriminately like a sea turtle. There were many one-night stands but no commitments. Neil's friends said he loved his boat more than any woman, and they were right.

"I've known many women," he said as he poured the last of the Haitian rum into Don's mug. "And I've known a lot of boats." He peered into the empty bottle and delved into a locker for another. "Island Girl is the best of them all," he mumbled. "She's been faithful to me for all these years, and that's more than any woman I've known."

The two friends had been drinking since early morning and Neil was waxing philosophical, a sure sign the rum was taking effect.

"A boat's not a living thing," Don insisted in a slurred voice while gesturing in the air. "Boats are just wood, iron, and canvas. Don't you want warmth and human passion?" He squeezed a lime into his mug and poured in rum. "Don't you see? It's right in front of you." Don put an unsteady hand on Neil's shoulder. "You've got it all. You've got Tula!"

Neil caressed the burnished tiller in silence. He knew Don meant well and was just trying to help.

"Were you ever married?" Don asked, attempting to change the subject.

Neil frowned and took a long drink. "Not that it's any of your business," he replied gruffly. "But yes, I was married once to a Swede." He took the empty rum bottle and attempted to pour another drink. When that failed, he added sugar to his mug and squeezed in a lime. Neil stood and raised his mug to the sky. "What the hell!" he shouted. "Nothing lasts forever and all rivers run to the sea. I love Tula and she loves me." He sat down hard and looked into the empty mug. "That's all that matters now," he muttered sadly.

"You're a drunken poet," Don said.

It was late and getting dark as Don pulled in the dinghy. "You sail at dawn," he said. "And I have to go home." They somehow managed to get into the dinghy without capsizing it and despite Don's condition, he sculled them ashore.

On the way, Neil became philosophical. "I've been a beachcomber all my life," he said. "I've stepped in globs of tar and felt it ooze between my toes." Don looked puzzled and stopped sculling. "It sure is messy," Neil mumbled. "But it feels kind of good, like what's between a woman's legs."

"Tar?" Don interrupted. "What's that got to do with a woman?"

"It's what John calls a metaphor," Neil explained in a slurred voice. "Don't you see? Women are the globs of tar between my toes."

Although dead drunk, Don was able to continue sculling. If they had capsized it would have sobered them up.

"That's the masochist in me," Neil continued. "It's a saving factor, because even bad things can be made good." He looked unsteadily at Don. "Do you dig what I'm saying?"

Don was laughing so hard he couldn't answer. "What about Tula?" he said. "She's certainly no glob of tar."

"You're absolutely correct," Neil mumbled. "Tula's not the tar between my toes. She's an immaculate seashell, a paper nautilus, a rare treasure for any collector."

They reached shore safely and Don stepped out of the dinghy. "Don't forget, my friend," he said. "Beaches come to an end if you walk far enough."

Neil was too hungover to leave the next morning. So, he slept in and spent the day with his friends at the club. That night, he took Tula aboard Island Girl and they made love until first light when he took her ashore and kissed her goodbye.

As the sun rose over Sandy Cay, Island Girl passed Fort Montague under full sail. When she reached Porgy Rocks, Neil set her on a course over the Yellow Banks. The voyage south was under way.

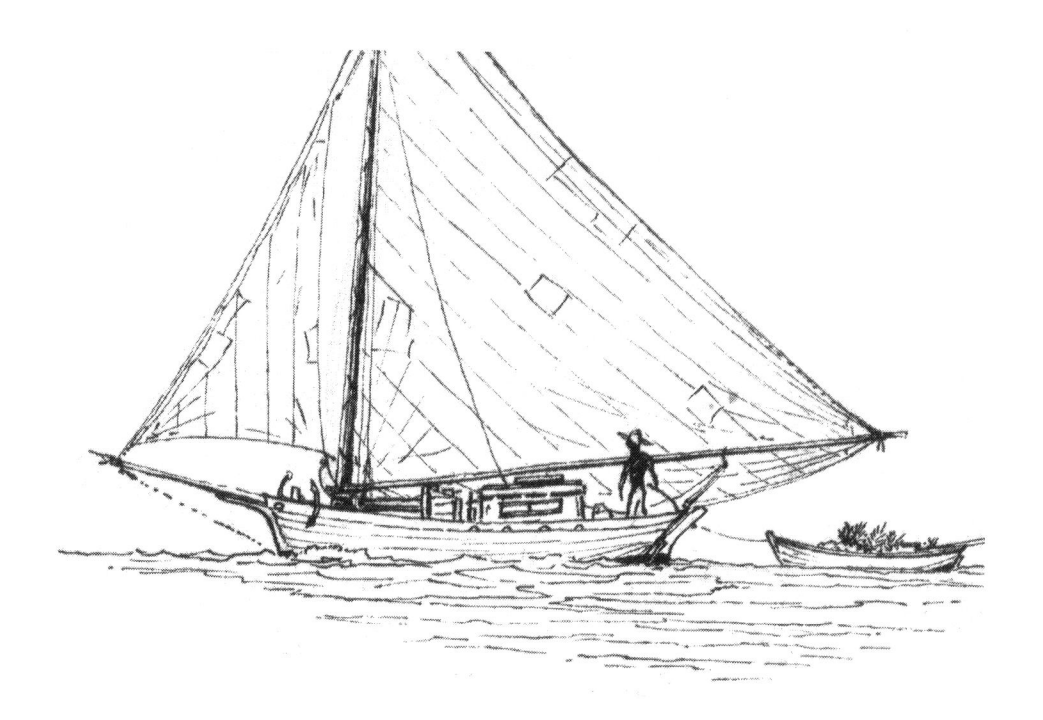

JAMAICA CREEK

Surging onto the shallows, it seemed as if Island Girl knew she was in her element. The lee deck was awash as she gathered way, breasting the tide rip where the banks and sea meet. The wind soon backed to the north.

"Perfect!" Neil thought, as he trimmed sails and steered for Binnacle Hill.

By sunset, Island Girl was skirting the mangrove-covered shore of Acklins Island. The wind had gone east and died away. So, Neil cranked the engine to life and motored close in under the lee of the land. There was a fathom of water over turtle grass and somewhere ahead was Jamaica Creek. Neil could not remember the landmarks for the creek. His notes of the area were in a log book back in Nassau. So he motored on relying on memory.

The steady chugging of the engine echoed back from the dark wall of mangroves to starboard. As darkness fell, Neil went forward to light the running lights. A heron rose from the mangroves with a raucous cry and at that moment, the mouth of Jamaica Creek opened up. Neil pushed the tiller to port and entered the creek. He saw a large motor vessel anchored far in back of the creek. As he came closer, he saw Maru lettered on the transom, tarpaulin-covered cargo on deck, and a radio mast lashed down by the deck house. Four men and a sad-eyed dog met him and stepped aboard when he brought Island Girl alongside.

A white man came forward, extending a hand. "I am Gabriel Vega, the captain of Maru." He was a man of about fifty, with gray hair and deep-set green eyes in a tanned and weathered face. He spoke with a Spanish accent. Although Neil sensed an aura of latent violence about him, he liked the man.

The vessel's crew consisted of three slightly-built Haitians, Rene, Oiseau, and Antoine. They spoke Creole among themselves and Spanish patois to the Captain. They were a well-knit crew, and it was evident that they got along well with the captain.

Cerberus, the sad-eyed dog, didn't growl or bark when Island Girl came alongside. Only when Neil came aboard did he raise his hackles. However, with Neil's love of animals, it wasn't long before man and beast were friends.

The first day in Jamaica Creek, the crew unloaded Island Girl's stone ballast to lighten her. After dumping a ton of ballast, they uncovered the Maru's deck cargo, exposing four wooden crates. They transferred them to Island Girl, where Neil had two placed on the cabin sole, forward of the engine and the others in line aft of the main mast. Battens were nailed to the sole and the crates were lashed down and covered with crocus sacks. The cargo was now the white man's responsibility. It was Neil Gardiner's problem.

Captain Vega turned to Neil, "She trims well."

Neil nodded, "It will be crowded down below, but what worries me is how light she'll be when those crates are gone."

"She will be a tender craft for sure. You will need to sail her easy," said Captain Vega.

In the late afternoon, everyone bathed in the creek and Neil speared three lobsters. That night, Oiseau cooked them in a spicy butter and rum sauce and served them at the mess table. After dinner, bottles of dark Haitian rum were set on the table and drinks were poured all around. Everyone was in a party mood after a day of hard work, a swim in the creek, and a hearty meal. A hissing pressure lamp lit the cabin and there was an odour of kerosene, salt-soaked wood, and engine oil. Neil relaxed and sat back, sipping his drink and looking around the cabin.

In front of him, there was the big mahogany mess table, its top scarred from years of hard use. There were hammocks hung on deck beams and a canvas-covered bunk bed. Above was a skylight through which a crescent moon shone. On the bulkhead nearby there was a ship's clock and a corroded barometer with a broken glass. On the inside sheer plank there were wooden pegs from which hung an assortment of clothing, sea bags, hanks of rope, and a pair of binoculars. On one peg, Neil noticed a leather belt with a holstered pistol.

After a few drinks, Captain Vega turned to Neil. "Do you know what is in those crates?"

"Whatever it is seems to require a lot of secrecy," Neil replied. "I wonder why you anchor so far up the creek and I notice you never raise the radio mast to transmit."

The Captain looked long and hard at Neil, took a sip of rum and said nothing.

Neil took a drink, "My guess is, it's guns and ammunition. The crates are the right size and weight." Then he added, "There are no markings on them."

"You may be correct," the Captain said, pouring more rum in his cup and leaning back against the bulkhead. "It could be weapons, but who knows?"

A crewman stood up and said something in Creole. The Captain made a gesture at him and turned to Neil. "Rene here says there will soon be trouble in Haiti. Do you know about Poppa Doc and Daniel Fignole?"

Neil nodded. "Yes, but the crates are bound for Cuba not Haiti."

The Captain grinned broadly and took another drink. "Soon there will be a need for weapons in Haiti," he said. "Listen to me, Captain Gardiner. There is money behind every revolution. Blood money!" He poured another drink. "Be advised!" he said, "Once you deliver those crates, you will be asked to deliver more. If you refuse, they will kill you."

"The men who pay us, who are they?" Neil asked, thinking of Ruiz and Escobar back in Nassau.

"They are not the ones who fight and die for a cause." The Captain took a long drink. "Cowards like Ruiz hold no beliefs and have no loyalty." The Captain snarled and pounded the table with an empty mug.

"So you know Ruiz?" asked Neil.

"Yes, he is the one of whom I speak. He sends us to supply the men who fight," replied Captain Vega.

Neil was taken aback by the Captain's anger. "I don't know about you," he said. "But I don't take chances, and I make damn good money."

The Captain frowned and leaned low across the table, His words were slurred but he spoke with concern. "You do not know the risk." he whispered.

"Perhaps I'll refuse to make another delivery if Ruiz asks me," said Neil.

"That would be unwise. Surely he will ask you to sail again." The Captain downed his drink, poured another and slammed his fist on the table, "Do Not Refuse!"

"It's the money!" Neil said. "It is too damn much and good to have." He shrugged his shoulders in resignation and looked squarely at the captain. "What is a man to do?"

"Do you believe in a cause?" Neil asked, trying to change the subject.

"I know nothing of the Cuban mountains. I'm a man of the sea," Captain Vega laughed aloud and began quoting a song. "I voyage for tarnished pesos on the unsailed wastes of unknown seas…." His head was on the table and Neil could hardly make out the slurred words. "If Ruiz wants you to make another trip," the captain mumbled and reached out for the rum bottle. His hand shook as he took it. "It will be your death to refuse." He stammered.

A crew member pushed a sugar bowl across to Neil. He had noticed the white man's habit of stirring sugar into the rum.

"Perhaps I will say no to my own padron" the captain muttered. "And perhaps I will not!"

"If Ruiz asks me again, I'll take a chance and refuse," Neil said. "I've grown a conscience talking with you."

The captain raised his head from the table, squinting at Neil through bloodshot eyes. "They will kill you. It has happened before." He lowered his head with a thud.

It was past midnight when Neil went back aboard Island Girl, cranked the engine to life and cast off. He motored a short way off and dropped anchor near a stand of mangroves. A heron flew up with a screech that echoed throughout the creek. Neil listened to the radio for a while, and after hearing a favorable weather report for the next day, he made a bed on top of the crates and fell asleep.

In the pre-dawn light, a cat's paw of wind bore Island Girl out of the creek. No one was on deck of the motor vessel when he motored past. As far as Neil knew, not even Cerebrus, the sad-eyed dog saw him leave.

As Island Girl moved from under the lee of the Island with the jib and mainsail set, Neil looked astern. A radio mast was rising above the mangroves. His departure had been noticed and it was being reported. Island Girl would be expected at Cayo Verde.

ABACO SLOOP

CAYO VERDE

Island Girl had been anchored for two days on the edge of the Gulf Stream in the dubious lee of Cayo Verde. It wasn't much of a lee. It was merely a scrub-covered rock where sea birds nested. At low tide the sandy shoals off Island Girl's stern were exposed and they afforded the only protection should the wind go east.

There had been no one there to meet me when I sailed in two days earlier. So, all I could do was wait. Ruiz had promised to be there and I was counting on him. The wind increased all afternoon, and with the full-moon high tide, there was an uncomfortable surge. I tied canvas around the anchor hawsers to prevent chafing and by afternoon it was worn through and had to be replaced.

As Island Girl rose and fell in the surge, I tied inner tubes in the bight of each hawser to dampen the strain on the anchors. When the tide changed, Island Girl began rolling and pitching and anything that wasn't secured went flying.

"Where the hell is Ruiz?" I wondered. At Jamaica Creek, they were ahead of schedule and waiting for me. "Island Girl can't take much more of this punishment," I thought. The constant strain on the ground tackle worried me. So, I set a third anchor and tied on more chafing gear. With such erratic movement it was impossible to sleep or cook a meal and it was difficult getting around the boat. All I could do was hold tight and wait for Ruiz.

The third night was even worse. The wind increased to gale force until midnight, when the tide changed and added to the confusion. I was on deck before dawn unable to sleep. I was considering leaving. Sailing across the banks at night would be dangerous, but I imagined how nice it would feel to be anchored safely somewhere else. It would mean an all-night sail with only moonlight to see the way through the shoals and reefs, but how good it would feel to be under sail again in a steady boat.

As I went forward to take in the anchors, a beam of light pierced the darkness and swept Island Girl from stem to stern. Over the sound of the pounding surf, I heard the throbbing of a Diesel engine and the rattle of anchor chain. The light went out and there were unintelligible shouts of command in the darkness.

I hoped it was Ruiz. Who else could it be? When my eyes adjusted from the glare of the searchlight, I saw a motor vessel anchored not twenty yards to starboard.

"It must be Ruiz," I murmured and went forward to inspect the chafing gear. When the rolling subsided somewhat, I went below and lit the stove and the anchor light. I put a kettle on to boil and hung the anchor light on the backstay above the companionway hatch. "They know I'm here," I thought. "So the anchor light really isn't necessary."

Back below, I sipped his tea and looked at the canvas-covered boxes crowding the cabin. "What the hell am I carrying?" I wondered. "Oh well, it's only three hours 'til dawn and then I'll be rid of them." I couldn't sleep so I opened a can of corned beef hash and had breakfast.

At first light, I was on the afterdeck washing dishes in a bucket of sea water. I could see that the motor vessel was a yacht, a nice-looking vessel with a high bow and a long run aft to a spacious cockpit. It had a tuna tower, a flying bridge, and fishing poles in sockets around the cockpit. By all appearances she was a seaworthy sports-fishing boat. She flew no flag and there were no names or numbers on the hull. Three men were doing something in the cockpit and another was on the bridge. It suddenly occurred to me that it might not be Ruiz at all, but some sport fishermen seeking shelter.

By noon the wind and seas subsided and the yacht weighed anchor and came alongside Island Girl. l threw out a line and it was caught by Ruiz.

He smiled at my surprise. "You did not expect me, eh Captain Gardiner?" he said. Ruiz was dressed in immaculate white slacks and a polo shirt, and he sported a fancy yachting cap. The only thing out of character was a two-day growth of beard. The three men with him were similarly dressed and had the same growth of beard. To all appearances, they were sportsmen on a fishing trip. When the boats were tied together with fenders between, Ruiz stepped aboard Island Girl.

"Let us commence," he said and turned to me. "You will help with the cargo transfer," he commanded.

l bristled. I didn't like taking orders from the little man, but I held my tongue and lent a hand. With the boats rolling and grinding against each other, it was a difficult job moving the heavy crates from Island Girl to the yacht.

All during the transfer, Ruiz stood by watching. Ruiz 'crew was not at all like the friendly Haitians I met at Jamaica Creek. They spoke Spanish and were obviously Latinos, probably Cuban. They seemed nervous and I noticed a Beretta in a holster at the small of one man's back. When all four crates were lashed down in the cockpit of the yacht, Ruiz gave me a limp handshake.

"Do not neglect the trip to Port-de-Paix," he said. "Your money will be in the bank when you return to Nassau."

As the yacht cast off, I stood in the companionway with only my head and shoulders showing. Out of sight, in my right hand was the Luger pistol fully loaded, cocked, and with the safety off. The yacht moved away, its diesels throbbing and then revving higher as it gathered speed, leaving Island Girl rolling in its wake. I watched as it rounded the cay and roared off into the angry Gulf Stream. I raised the Lugar, switched on the safety, withdrew the clip, and ejected a cartridge from the chamber. I breathed a sigh of relief as I took down the anchor light and unfurled the sails. Now that the crates were gone, there was a difference in the pitch and roll. "They'll be where they're going and back in Nassau before I'm half way home," I thought.

On a broad reach from under the lee, Island Girl breasted a rip tide and cleared the shoals. By dawn, we were past the reef and under sail in blue water. I said a prayer of thanks and set a course for the salt island of Great Exuma to pick up rock ballast.

RENATA, THE FIRST MEETING

The Captain said Ruiz would surely want me to make other deliveries. So since I valued my life, I was on my way to Cuba with crates of rifles for Che's contingent.

I was met at Baracoa by an American-educated Cuban. "Call me Javi," he said, extending a hand. "I brought help for the cargo," he said, gesturing behind at four men and two mules.

It was a long hot trek from Baracoa to the base of Monte Alba, where we began a climb to the top.

As I stood on the summit catching my breath, a beautiful young girl approached and offered me a cup of coffee. She moved in close, gazing up at my face with slanted brown eyes, the eyes of a Sibonay Indian.

"Renata," a man's voice commanded. "Come! Do not bother the boy. He has been on a long journey from the islands. He must rest and catch his breath." Javi mumbled, smiling.

"Ah ha," I thought. "Now I know her name."

An elderly white-haired gentleman stood in the shade of a giant banyan tree. He was dressed in faded khakis and his goatee was tobacco-stained. I assumed he was the girl's father.

She averted her gaze and ran from me, shouting, "But Poppi, he has green eyes!" Laughter erupted from the men unloading the mules. The girl ran to the man under the tree, her buttocks flexing and her long legs nimble in the sunlight. When I turned to look at the laughing men one of them was glaring at me with undisguised hatred.

Javi was watching nearby. He sidled up to me. "That's Rudolfo," he whispered. "Watch out for him."

Rudolfo was known by the men on the summit as a volpe, and for good reason. He had no respect for women and even less for a girl of sixteen like Renata. She was the only female on Monte Alba and consequently an object of desire.

Renata would have nothing to do with Rudolfo. She ignored his crude advances and avoided him whenever possible. The only thing keeping Rudolfo from her was her father, Eos.

The men on Monte Alba were a tough group of young revolutionaries; cane cutters from the lowlands and fishermen from the coast. Unlike Rudolfo, they respected Renata and treated her as they would a mother or a sister. They called her by name, but in private they referred to her as Brujita.

"Why do they call her Brujita?" I asked Javi.

"She does things. She has powers," he replied and quickly changed the subject.

The first day was spent unpacking the rifles and securing the ammunition. Next day we set up a firing range and I taught the men how to strip and reassemble the M-1 carbines. Then I showed them how to load, aim, and fire with magazines taped in opposition. They were an eager group and learned quickly.

That first night on Monte Alba I dreamed of Renata, of her lovely face and her Indian eyes. Suddenly I felt warm breath on my face, lips pressing mine, and a softness against my chest. I awoke with a throbbing erection and my arms around a woman's naked body. Strong arms held me close.

"Be still," a voice whispered, and my erection pierced a tight, warm wetness. I awoke at dawn wondering if I had been raped by a succubus.

Later that day, Renata came from her hut and walked up to me. "You look tired Gringo," she said with an amused grin, "Did you not sleep well?" Her eyes sparkled with mischievous delight as she turned and sauntered away. So it wasn't a wet dream after all. Renata had come in the night and made love to me.

The next night she came again but not in a dream. With a flourish, she threw open the tent flaps and crawled into bed beside me. This time, I was fully awake and ready for her.

From that day on we were lovers and spent every night and most days together. Our affair continued despite Poppi's disapproval of me and dislike of Gringos in general. It was only after I rescued Renata from Rudolfo that Poppi accepted me as his daughter's lover.

Renata and I met in the forest and on the grassy hillsides. We got to know each other in all the ways of lovers. Our bodies merged and we came together as a single entity like the beings in Plato's Aristophenes. We existed in an erotic fantasy world as the only two people on earth.

After I made another trip with arms and supplies from the Bahamas, the men built a hut for Renata and me on the Summit. To satisfy Renata, I joined the revolution and got to know Che, doctor Granados, and most of the Sierra Maestra contingent.

I had been on the summit for four months when I awoke one morning to the sound of scuffling and Renata's troubled voice. Rushing out, I found her struggling with Rudolfo who had his arms around her.

I delivered a blow to his spine. He released her and turned to me with a knife in his hand. After I delivered a reflexive blow to the gut, he dropped the knife and fell to his knees in pain. Javi stepped in and picked up the knife.

In the background, I heard Renata laughing and crying hysterically. I leaned down and shouted in Rudolfo's ear, "If you touch her again I will kill you!" Javi handed him the knife and repeated in Spanish what I had just said in English.

Some time later, I began running messages and doing surveillance for Che. It was surprisingly easy. I roamed the island as a tourist and sometimes I was taken for a Russian.

After the incident with Rudolfo, there was no more trouble until later when he told the Eschevarias that I had turned their son over to Batista's police.

One day I came upon Renata sitting on a rock in the woods. A bird was flying circles around her head and there were lizards and a tortoise at her feet. As I approached, the bird flew away, the lizards scattered, and the tortoise pulled into its shell.

"I felt you coming," she said without turning to look at me. That was my first awareness of my lover's psychic powers and why the men called her Brujita.

POPPI

In 1930, revolution was in the air in Catalonia. War clouds were building and a young man by the name of Eos Soura wanted no part of it. He set sail in a small boat singing, "Adieu and farewell Spanish lady. Farewell Ladies of Spain!"

Weeks later he made landfall in Cuba, where he met and married a Siboney Indian woman.

A year later she died in childbirth, leaving Eos with a baby daughter he named Renata.

THE MESSAGE

"You look like a cane cutter," Carlos said with his hand on my shoulder. "A Cuban cane-break worker for sure, but you don't *smell* like one." Carlos added, and everyone laughed.

It was February and the cane fields were burning. We were gathered together by lantern light in Che's hut, Just the five of us. There was Che, the comandante; Juanito, the student of all disciplines; Mexican Carlos, one of six La Playa survivors; my friend Javier, and me. Uninvited, Rudolfo lounged in the doorway listening.

"What about his eyes?" Javier asked, gesturing at me. "A cane cutter with *green* eyes?" he said derisively.

"And his hands," Carlos said, displaying his palms to Che. "They have no calluses. His hands betray him."

"Neil is the best man to carry the message," Che growled, clenching his fists. "He may be a Gringo, but he's loyal to our cause."

Che looked around the room, his eyes resting briefly on each man's face. *"So he will carry the message to the Escambrays and meet with Carlos Antonio."* That was that! Che had made a decision.

At first light, Javi awakened me and we walked downhill into the encampment. Carlos was there with his wife and older brother who were to accompany us as far as Cuernala.

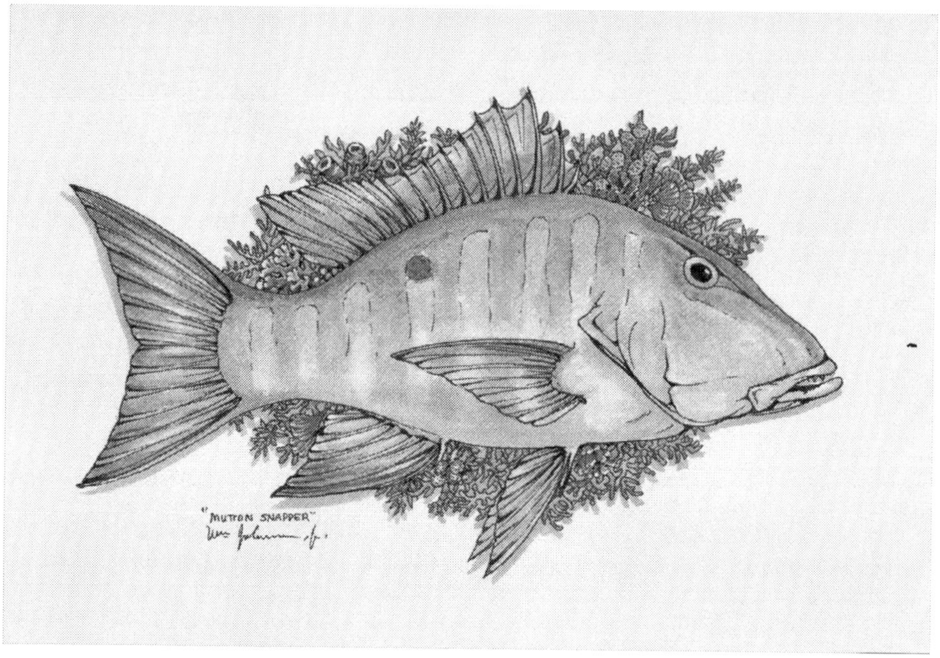
"MUTTON SNAPPER"

ESCAMBRAYS

"Don't go," Renata said. "He can send someone else."

I explained that it had to be me. "I'm an American, a Gringo," I said. "And I'm the only one who can play the part of a tourist. Besides, Che ordered it."

"It is not safe," Renata insisted. "Your face is known, and there are traitors among us here in the mountains."

When I couldn't be dissuaded, she held me close and cried. It did no good. That night she tried everything to make me change my mind, but at dawn I walked down the hill to Juanito waiting in the truck.

It was a hot afternoon when we pulled up to the bus station in Santa Clara. A soldier with a Garand rifle slung on his shoulder and sergeant's stripes painted on his shirt sleeves motioned me through.

"Venga Yankee!" he snarled.

"Good," I thought. "I'm being seen as a tourist."

As the truck drove away, I stepped onto a crowded bus.

"Hola, Ruskie!" the driver shouted, extending a hand in comradely greeting.

"An even better recognition. He thinks I'm a Russian!"

"Da, gracias!" I said and took a seat beside an Indian woman with a kid goat in her lap. She smiled and offered me a mint.

It was a long, hot drive across the savannah, past burned-out sugar cane fields and into the Escambray foothills. That night with the bus winding its way into the hills, we slept with our heads covered from the night air. I listened to the snores and murmured nightmares of my fellow passengers as the bus bounced along the pot-holed road. Suddenly a gunshot rang out and the bus screeched to a stop.

Back-lit by a fire on the road ahead, two soldiers with drawn pistols entered the bus. They went about uncovering the face of each passenger as if looking for someone. When the soldiers came to me, the Indian woman said something in Spanish and they passed me by with barely a glance. As the bus drove away past the fire, the woman turned to me with a triumphant grin and she winked.

Did she know who I was, and that I was scheduled to meet with Jose Eschevaria the next day?

BETRAYAL BY RUDOLFO

By June, sympathy for the revolution was widespread and it was supported island-wide by the people. There were two camps of revolutionaries, Che's comrades in the Sierra Maestras and Jose Antonio Escheveria's in the Escambrays. During the past year, I had delivered many messages and small items from Che to Jose Antonio, and I made a second delivery of weapons from the Bahamas. It was easy. I roamed the island unimpeded as a tourist and sometimes I was mistaken for a Russian.

I was returning to the Sierra Maestras after delivering Che's latest message. I was having breakfast in Rio Luna when I heard that Jose had been captured and was going to be executed the next day. Because of his attempted assassination of Batista, the manhunt for him had been intense.

Later that day, I heard that Jose's family was accusing me of turning in their son. They were calling for my death. I could not believe that the Escheverias, who knew me as Jose's friend, could think that I had betrayed him.

After Jose's execution, Eloy Menoyo formed the Escambray Alliance, and to fill the gap, Jose's men joined him. Revolution, like water, seeks its own level.

Che composed a letter to Eloy Menoyo vowing support and extolling their mutual desire to depose Batista. Despite being under a death threat, I was chosen to deliver the message. I was confident that the death threat would be ignored by the people. Javi accompanied me to the Alliance camp and I gave the message to Eloy. In the camp I learned the reason for the Eschiverias' death threat.

Rudolfo, out of jealousy of my affair with Renata, had convinced them I had betrayed their son. When I told Javi of Rudolfo's treachery, he frowned, "Es malvado! Something will have to be done."

That afternoon I met Rudolfo and I confronted him. The next day it was as if he had never existed. I continued on alone to the Sierra Maestras, ignoring the death threat, but when I got off the bus in Cardenas someone took a shot at me and missed. There was panic in the bus station as everyone ran for cover. A volley of shots rang out and I dove for cover behind a wall. "That's an automatic weapon," I thought. "Things are getting serious."

I found my way on foot to the next town where I knew there was a family loyal to the revolution. The trouble was that it was dark and I didn't know how to find them. I was startled by a voice behind me in the dark. "Hola Gringo, que pasa?" It was the Indian woman I sat next to on the Escambray bus. She helped me then, and she helped me again by leading me to the loyalists' house. The people there took me in without question and sequestered me for a year. They were a family of four, a mother, father, and two daughters: Elisia the chaste, and Guapita the golfa.

AFFAIR WITH GUAPITA

I wondered why Guapita lived away from her parents as if she was disowned. They considered her a golfa, a whore, and I soon found out why.

Guapita was addicted to sexual intercourse and she was extremely good at it. In fact, she indulged in it shamelessly. After embarking on an affair with her, I discovered she was a pleasure-seeking hedonist with a vengeful alter-ego she called Esclavita, who demanded punishment for sexual pleasures. The punishments were cruel and long-lasting. At times Gaupita remained hogtied all day until her sister found and freed her.

When I was in charge, the bondage was never cruel and always brief. Guapita's room away from home was a spacious place, tile floored, with a beamed ceiling and white stucco walls. There were two doorways, the front door and an access door to a lavatory and shower. There was a straight back wooden chair, a large comfortable bed, a foot locker, and little else.

A casual observer might have wondered why there were ring bolts in the ceiling beams and why there were shoes with high stiletto heels under the bed. In the foot locker, there were coils of shibari rope and an assortment of leather straps and belts. There was also a bag containing clothespins and a knobby rubber dildo. Under it all, as if hidden in shame, was a horse whip. The contents of the locker were exclusively Esclavita's.

When I first met Guapita, I wondered why she got so stoned on only one shot of brown vodka. She acted as if she had smoked pot all day. When she told me the brown vodka was a tincture of hashish I understood and joined her in a drink. That was the first time we had sex and it was the start of an intense affair. I soon learned to satisfy the Esclavita side of Guapita with shibari bondage and other methods of restraint.

The last day we were together, I fucked Guapita long and hard until Esclavita appeared demanding, "Atara me, Atara me!" So I did her bidding and tied-up the libidinous vamp, left her in bondage, and walked away knowing her sister would untie her later.

On the street, in the guise of a tourist, I strolled past a soldier who glared at me with a finger on the safety of his Kalashnikov. Ahead, a couple walked hand in hand to a night of carnal pleasure. A rat scurried across my foot pursued by a well-fed cat. There was a squeak, a quick death, and then silence in the twilight. The sky darkened. Night was nigh.

Suddenly the stillness was pierced by the lusty notes of a flamenco lullaby. As I walked, my thoughts turned to Renata in the mountains, to Renata the consummate lover, and to Brujita the psychic. I wondered if I really loved her, or if it was only lust. Was I still searching for a perfect woman? Surely there was friendship with Renata. Her desires were many and varied mine. Her lust was strong. Above all, I feared her psychic powers.

Renata, as Brujita, had the ability to create and control dreams. The first time we made love, she imbued my dream with her physical presence. It was so real that it pleasured me more than any woman ever had. Since then, she has given me only romantic erotic dreams, never nightmares. So perhaps I should not fear her powers.

Once in a hashish-induced state, Brujita told my fortune. She said that at a future time I would meet the perfect woman and my life long quest would be at an end. "And," she added with a triumphant grin, "You will be a Viejo and unable to satisfy a woman."

At the time, I took Brujita's prediction of unattainable lust as a woman's natural jealousy. Little did I know that in my waning years I would meet a perfect woman, Rachael, and the prediction would come true.

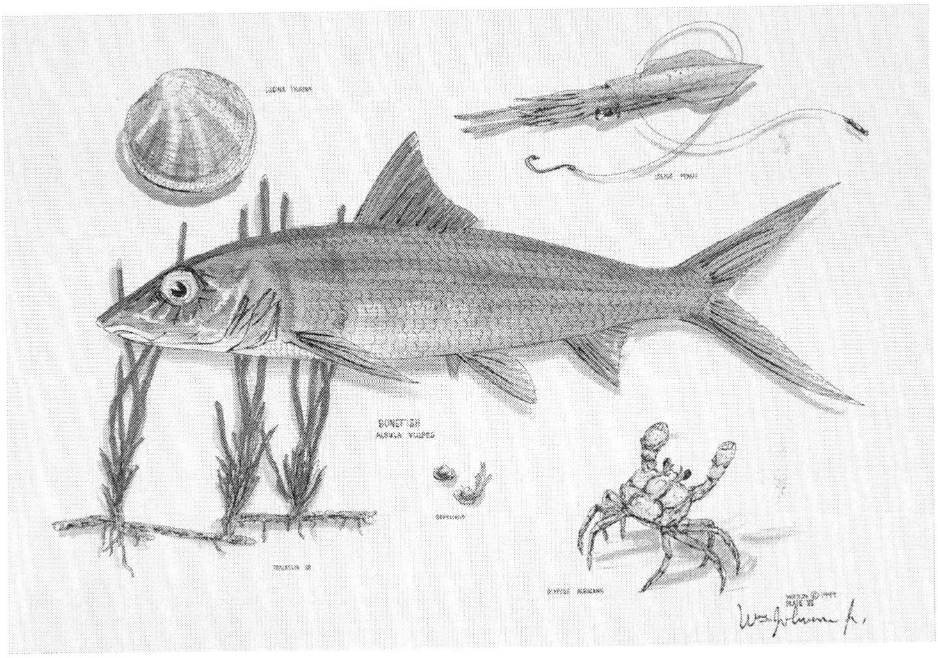
BONEFISH

NOSTALGIA

Between thunder claps, she dances for me in heels to the tune of an old Latin love song, Quisas
Her body writhes in sensual harmony with the music, promising that when the dance ends there will be love.

Perhaps, perhaps
Windows rattle,
Rain pounds the roof
Bodies entwine,
There's sanctuary between her legs
And pleasure deep within her

Was it Shari or Renata who danced for me, or was it a dream?

LONG ROAD TO HAVANA

At the time I didn't know it, but it was to be my last trip to Cuba. This time it was with medical supplies for Doctor Granados. When the harbour master assigned Island Girl a mooring in Baracoa Harbour, he told me the revolution had succeeded. Castro had declared victory and was on his way to confront Batista in Havana.

Since I was still being hunted, I decided not to go to Havana. I understood why the Escheverias might suspect me of betraying their son. It didn't take much for Rudolfo to convince them. He knew of my frequent visits to the Escambray camp and that I was familiar with the security there. They believed him and I could not convince them otherwise.

As the weeks passed their anger turned to vengeance, and a manhunt for me was under way. Even some who were loyal to the revolution believed Rudolfo. I was on the run from both friend and foe. Corsicans are known for their impulsive vendettas, but Basque vendettas are about family honor and they can last for generations.

The Escheverias were Mexican with ancestral roots in the Pyrenees Alps. Later I was to learn that the person who shot at me was not some gullible citizen who believed I was a traitor, but a hired assassin sent by the family to kill me. Luckily he was a bad shot.

The day we left the safety of Che's mountains to deliver the letter to Eloy Menoyo I was fired on again. Javi just laughed and said, "The guy's a lousy shot."

LOVERS

Neil and Shari checked into a hotel in the Tacubaya District of Mexico City and took a taxi to the far end of Avenida Reforma, where it intersects with Avenida Juarez. There they left the taxi and walked to Alameda Park with its maze of paths and green cast iron fences.

At the Juarez monument Neil said, "Shari, there's something I want to show you." He took her hand and they continued along the sidewalk by the park. Suddenly Shari stopped with a gasp. Inside the iron fence was a life-size marble sculpture of a woman chained hand and foot. She was in a crawling position with her head turned toward them. There was despair on the sculptured face, but Shari saw something more.

"There's ecstasy and defiance in those marble eyes." she said. Shari took Neil's arm and drew him close.

"She's very much me, don't you think?" she whispered and asked, "Who's the sculptor?"

"I don't know." Neil answered, "But whoever it was, he set a mood with his chisel. He carved an esoteric fantasy for others of like mind."

"Like us." Shari murmured and kissed Neil on the cheek.

As they walked away Neil turned to her. "You may be a Leo," he said, "But you'll always be Andromeda to me."

Shari laughed. "You're certainly no Perseus," she replied. "You'd never release me from my chains."

"Not from those you choose to wear," he smirked. "There's something else I want you to see," he said, motioning ahead. "It's something quite different."

They crossed the Avenida and entered the marble hall of the Palacio de Bellas Artes. They took the stairs to the upper atrium gallery and Neil led Shari to one side. He put a hand on her shoulder and turned her to face the opposite wall. There was a gigantic Orozco painting of a chained woman in a distorted perspective reaching out from a fiery blood-red background. The emotional impact of the painting struck Shari. She shivered and turned away

"It's too much contrast," she whispered. Shari searched for words, became angry, and raised her voice. "First, you show me that beautiful marble statue with its erotic sensitivity, and now *This,*...this out-of-proportion insult to the senses. Even the colours are insulting," she growled as they descended to the lobby.

Neil was smiling because he had known what Shari's reaction would be to the Orozco painting.

"What the hell are you smiling at?" Shari snapped angrily.

The next day, they returned to the Bella Artes and Neil sat Shari on a bench in front of Camarena's mural of the conquest of Mexico.

"Think of this, my love," he said, blocking her view of the mural. "You appreciated the sculpture in the park. Then you hated the Orozco painting. It was too much contrast for one day, and I apologize. Now, I want you to see a painting that I love." Neil stepped aside.

Shari gazed in awe at the Camarena mural. Its execution and brilliantly rendered details stunned her into silent wonder. The mural was realistic in detail and colour and replete with Aztec folklore and imagery. Its overpowering beauty set a mood of tranquility for both Neil and Shari.

"I knew you'd like it," Neil said when he saw Shari smile. They spent the morning studying the mural, and when they stepped out onto the Avenida Juarez it was late afternoon.

"Let's walk back to the hotel," Neil suggested. "There's something more I want you to see." They strolled the Reforma, that great double-lane boulevard bisecting Mexico City. Shari noticed how people looked only ahead or down at the ground, not at the sky. Neil, on the other hand, being a sailor looked up and scanned the sky for birds and weather signs.

They left the Reforma at Cuernos and walked the back streets of the Tacubaya district, stopping at a small shop to buy cups of cold yogurt. The shop owner, an elderly lady, remembered Neil and welcomed him with an embrace and kisses. Shari was impressed with the woman's energy and later with her command of four languages, but what impressed her most were the dogs. The shop had no door. A number of dogs lay sprawled about on the floor and outside on the sidewalk. Men passing by raised their hats in respect to the Senora and detoured around the dogs onto the street. Passers by smiled and waved to her and no one seemed to mind the dogs.

"She's one of my favorite people in the world," Neil said as they walked away eating yogurt in paper cup.

"What's the senora's name?" Shari asked.

"Anna Maria de laTorre," Neil replied. "Her parents fled Russia during the Bolshevik revolution." Neil smiled. "She was born here in Mexico but she claims to be Russian. She works part time as an interpreter for the Federal Police."

Neil paused for a moment grinning. "Can you believe it? She feeds all those dogs and knows each one's name? The Senora is a thoroughly good person," he added.

"If I'd seen only her dogs," Shari replied, "I would have known that."

NOTE: Mexico City has more statues than any city in the World. They range from bronze to marble and most of them are of historic figures. However the statue of the chained woman was an exception.

Have You Ever

Have you ever revisited a city or a country where you were once in love and very happy? It's almost always disappointing, because time and progress have taken their toll. The places have changed and so have we.
When we were young and in love, all was right with the world. Love and romance were primary, immediate, and overpowering. Now, when we revisit those venues of joy, it's all gone. The world is no longer what it was and *we* are not as we were.

TEPOZTECO

The next week, before driving to the coast, the lovers made a visit to Tepoztlan. Tepoztlan is a Mexican town about fifteen miles from the city of Cuernavaca, in the state of Morelos. At one time it was a study area for ethnologists and anthropologists because the people there hold fast to ancient customs and religions. Curanderos and brujos exist there as everyday facts of life, not two miles from the super highway from Mexico City to Acapulco.

High above the town, on a rocky pinnacle there is a temple in the form of a small pyramid. It is dedicated to Tepoztecatl, the god of pulque and debauchery. It is called Tepozteco and is held sacred by the people. There is a yearly pilgrimage to the pyramid. Every year lives are lost. There are white crosses in the arroyo where people have fallen.

The day before leaving Cuernavaca for the Pacific coast, the lovers drove to Tepoztlan. Shari packed three bottles of wine, some brown bread, and goat cheese in a knapsack while Neil rented a car for the day. It was ten o'clock by the time they reached the Tepoztlan and made their way through the market day crowds. They parked the car at the entrance of a narrow arroyo that leads up to the temple. As they entered the arroyo, the glare and aridness of the valley behind them turned to humid shade. The path was steep and narrow with moss-covered boulders and rocks washed by rivulets of water from springs higher up. The cloying odour of rotting vegetation was in the air as the lovers made their way.

"Every year, there's a pilgrimage here and there's a Bacchanal above, on the pyramid." Neil said as he helped Shari over a boulder. "The people come to give thanks to Tepoztecatl, the god of pulque and debauchery." He handed Shari his knapsack and climbed over a fallen tree.

As they ascended, the walls of the arroyo narrowed forming a rock-strewn gorge with high walls on either side. Rivulets from springs above lent the sounds of drips and cascades to the dank stillness.

"It doesn't look like anyone has been here in ages." Shari said as she paused to catch her breath.

"The festival was three months ago," Neil said, "And not many tourists come this far off the beaten track. The locals have no reason to come here. So I guess we're the only ones."

Shari looked at the steep trail ahead and at the high rock walls on either side of them. "This place has a strange feel. There's an aura of age and death here, like it's full of spirits." She frowned and turned to Neil. "Am I being too spooky?" she asked.

"Not at all! You caught the mood very well. There *are* spirits here, and they aren't tranquil." He motioned her ahead. "Remind me to tell you about them when we reach the top."

They came to a sheer rock wall at the end of the gorge, and Neil, having been there before, took Shari into a crevasse where a ladder led up to the next stage of the climb. "This will be the most dangerous part of our ascent," Neil announced as they climbed the ladder. "There's a narrow path above that skirts a six-hundred-foot drop off. So be careful! Every year people fall to their deaths from it."

Earlier, they had passed white crosses on the path below with names inscribed on them. Shari shivered thinking those must be the spirits she felt. "The idea of the festival," Neil explained, "Is to make the climb, sit on the pyramid, drink pulque, and praise Tepoztecatl. Then try to descend alive." He gave a grin. "The descent is at night and the people carry torches and sing. It's quite a sight from below in the town" Neil chuckled, "It's a matter of survival. Some people make it home to nurse hangovers, and others are laid out dead in the Spanish church."

"Natural selection!" Shari said thoughtfully. "The town down there must be made up of the best breed of mountain climbers in Mexico."

"That's a theory worthy of Charles Darwin," Neil said. "You may be onto something. It's been going on for centuries and the surefooted have survived to breed more. Some scientist should do a study on that."

The last rung of the ladder brought them onto a path leading around the base of the pinnacle. On the summit, the lovers peered down at the town of Tepoztlan below. It was market day, and from their perspective, the throngs of people looked like scurrying ants. Neil pointed to the great escarpment in the distance and explained that it enclosed the Valley of Mexico. Far beyond the escarpment the peaks of two volcanoes showed above the clouds. They prompted Neil to tell Shari the Aztec legend of Popocatepetl, the guardian warrior and Iztaccihuatl, the sleeping princess.

The lovers sat atop the pyramid, drinking wine while ambient music floated up from the valley below. They wondered how it must have felt in ancient times for an Aztec about to be sacrificed.

Shari shivered. "Why do I feel only one spirit up here?" She asked.

"The spirits you felt below were those of fallen worshipers." Neil explained. "Ancient sacrifices were made right here on this altar, but their spirits and those below are overpowered by that of a chief named Mixcoatl. He's similar to Theseus in Greek mythology, and we're sitting on his grave."

Shari stood up, "Shit! You mean someone is buried here?"

"Yes," Neil explained. "Ce Acatl was the orphaned son of a great chief who grew up in Tepoztlan with his maternal grandparents. He grew to become a priest and an even greater chief than his father. Later, he became the earthly embodiment of the Toltec god, Quetzalcoatl. Ce Acatl's family is steeped in legend," Neil continued. "His father, Mixcoatl, took the place of a sacrificial victim and was swallowed by a dragon-beast, but with a copper knife he cut his way out and killed the beast, thus freeing his people from the annual sacrifice. Later, while hunting in the valley below, Mixcoatl was surprised by a beautiful woman he mistook for a deer. He loosed two arrows at her and she deflected them with her hand. He named the woman Chimalma and took her to his kingdom in the north."

Shari was listening with rapt attention. "What does her name mean?" she asked.

"Chimalma means Shield Hand in the Toltec language." Neil explained and continued. "She became pregnant by swallowing a jade bead but she died giving birth to a son, Ce Acatl. At the moment of Ce Acatl's birth, Mixcoatl was killed by an assassin. The child was raised in Tepoztlan and he grew to become a priest of the god Quetzalcoatl. Later he was called to rule the Toltec nation, but before he took on the task, he found his father's bones and built this temple to house them. After that he sought out and killed his father's assassin in an epic battle. He freed his people, traveled north, founded the city of Tula, and ruled there in peace and prosperity for twenty years."

"There has to be a tragic end to that story." Shari said. "You know what I mean? Some sort of Freudian realization, or an ironic twist of fate…Something like that."

"Oh yes," Neil replied. "But it was a long time coming and it spanned the centuries. You might say that Ce Acatl influenced Mexican history and was responsible for the coastal Indians accepting Cortez as the embodiment of Quetzalcoatl."

"Just another example of the Buddhist fan-shaped destiny," Shari commented. "Mexican history sure is complicated!"

"There's more," Neil said. "All of this was set in motion by a sorcerer-priest named Tezcatlipoca…"

"What does that name mean in Toltec?" Shari interrupted.

"It means something like 'Smoky Mirror.' Anyhow, this Tezcatlipoca was jealous of Ce Acatl's power, and he…"

"Don't you mean Quetzalcoatl's power?" Shari interrupted again.

"They were the same." Neil answered. "Ce Acatl was the earthly embodiment of Quetzalcoatl. At any rate, the sorcerer-priest sent a beautiful woman to seduce Ce Acatl and persuade him to drink pulque."

"That's not so bad. He could get drunk and laid at the same time." Shari quipped.

"During Ce Acatl's reign," Neil continued ignoring her, "He vowed to abstain from sex and drink and to promote all forms of self-improvement. In many ways his outlook was Buddhist in nature. He was attempting to lead the Toltec nation onto something like the ten-fold path. Ce Acatl believed strongly in the duality of humanity and nature, that good and evil, as well as male and female, exist within each of us, and that the gods maintain the balance. It's a Yang-Yin philosophy."

"So, did he fuck the woman and drink Pulque?" Shari asked.

"Oh, yes! Being human, he gave way to his weaknesses. He was seduced and drank the pulque. That was Ce Acatl's undoing and the downfall of ancient Mexico."

"What happened to Ce Acatl?" Shari asked.

"In remorse and shame, he destroyed much of what he had built, buried his vast treasure of gold and jade, and took a band of misfits with him out of the valley of Mexico. They traveled past the sacred volcanoes and down to Vera Cruz on the coast. There, it's said he built a raft of snakes, the symbols of Quetzalcoatl, and they sailed away to the east never to be seen again."

"Yes!" Shari exclaimed, remembering the story of Cortez. "That all fits in with the legend. When Cortez arrived at Vera Cruz from the east, the Indians thought he was their god, Quetzalcoatl."

"What's also interesting," Neil added, "Is that the Mayans had a legend of a god arriving from the east with the rising sun. They called him Kukulcan. He was revered just like Quetzalcoatl. Kukulcan's symbol was also a serpent, the feathered serpent."

When Neil finished, they sat for a while in silence looking out over the valley at the distant mountains.

"So we're sitting here over the bones of chief Mixcoatl." Shari said. "No wonder I feel a spirit around me."

"That's the legend." Neil said. "And this is the hill of the star in Aztec mythology. The same star, Venus, is associated with their god from the east."

"So much history." Shari said.

As the lovers sat eating, drinking, and listening to sounds from the town below, a bird flew up from the valley in effortless spirals, hovered a moment and flew away. Neil laid back, looked up at the sky and raised a half empty wine bottle. "A jug of wine, a loaf of bread, and thou beside me." He recited.

"Ok, Omar, don't get stupid. This is no wilderness." Shari leaned over and put her arms around Neil. "I want to spend the night here with you," she said as she pulled him close. "I'll be the Princess and you be the Guardian who fucks her."

Neil wondered how it might be to make love there on the pyramid under the stars. The thought of having Shari in such a place of reverence and violence excited him. He pushed her down gently and laid between her legs. A warrior spirit watched with green jade eyes and shell teeth, and it shook a rattle in time with the lovers' pelvic thrusts.

Later that afternoon, Neil told Shari, "We can't spend the night up here. It'll be windy and cold and we have no bedding. We'd better start down now before the sun sets. The descent is more dangerous than the climb.

Shari was repacking the knapsack when they heard voices. Neil was suddenly alert. He ran to the edge of the pinnacle and looked down. Two people were coming up the narrow path below. They carried backpacks and wore ponchos over their shoulders in Mexican fashion.

"They walk like hill Indians," Neil thought. From his view, he could not see their faces, but one of them appeared to be a woman.

"Come, Shari! We'll start down now," Neil spoke in an urgent whisper.

They began the descent knowing they were no longer alone. Half way along the path they came face to face with the two strangers. One was an Indian of perhaps sixty, tall for a man of that region, with a lean body and a badly-scarred face. The other was a tall dark eyed woman with her raven hair gathered up under a straw hat. Neil noticed how strikingly beautiful she was. There was something familiar about her, something he couldn't quite put his finger on. Her well-sculpted mouth, the aquiline nose and prominent cheekbones, everything but her cold dark eyes reminded him of someone. But who? There was an aura about the woman that contrasted with her beauty, and it disturbed Neil. He had seen it right away but he could not define it.

Both parties stood for a moment looking at each other. It was obvious the strangers had not expected to see another couple there. After his first impression of the woman, Neil kept his eyes on the Indian who had his left hand under his poncho. Shari and the woman looked at each other without speaking or smiling. The Indian had been staring intently at Neil and he broke the silence. "Don Rojas," he said questioningly. "Que tal, compadre? Que paso?"

The woman made a sharp cutting gesture. "Silencio, Cazador!" she hissed. The Indian went silent, but kept his eyes on Neil.

"You must excuse us." The woman said to Shari. "My friend has been drinking and he is most confused. He mistook your husband for another." She smiled for the first time, and though it was a lovely smile, it gave Neil a chill. He looked back at the Indian who stood silent with a confused expression. His hand remained under his poncho.

Shari stepped forward. "We are on our way down," she said, smiling with a gesture at the path ahead. "The summit is yours."

"Walk carefully," the woman said, motioning for them to pass.

Neil motioned for Shari to go first and he waited until the Indian leaned back against the cliff wall to let her pass. He jumped ahead landing behind her in a crouch. He looked back at the strangers and saw fear in the Indian's eyes.

The woman laughed. "You are somewhat of a mountain goat," she said approvingly. Shari glared back at her.

"I know you from somewhere," Neil replied. "Have we met before?"

The woman smiled again, a lovely whiteness in a tan and weathered face. "At first you too looked familiar," she replied and shrugged her shoulders. "But that happens much in my life. All handsome men seem familiar to me." She looked defiantly at Shari who stood tense and silent behind Neil. The woman turned to the Indian. "Venga, Cazador. Andale!" she shouted as one might to a burro, and they started up the path.

As the lovers made their way down in silence, Neil's head was filled with the sounds of gongs and bugles mixed with human voices in an alien language. As they drove back to Cuernavaca, Shari broke the silence.

"That old Indian thought he knew you," she said, staring at the road ahead. Neil was silent for a while trying to collect his thoughts.

"The woman said he was drunk, but I don't think so. Did you notice he kept his hand under his poncho the whole time?"

"His left hand!" Shari added and looked ahead at the road. "What a strange couple they were. Such a beautiful woman, and he was so ugly! And wasn't it odd what she said about handsome men?" Neil laughed but said nothing. So, Shari continued, "That's what I've always said about you and beautiful women. They all look familiar to you."

Shari stared out the window at the parched fields of the high valley and mumbled, "I wonder what they were doing there so late in the day?"

"Probably the same thing we talked about," Neil answered, "Spending the night and making love on the pyramid. They must have had bed rolls in those backpacks."

Neil turned his attention to the road ahead with thoughts of the woman, and how the sinistral Indian had mistaken him for another. What had the woman called the Indian? Was it Cazador?

That night in Cuernavaca, Neil awoke to find Shari beside him with her hands exploring his body. Sleep turned to lust and they made love. In the morning, Shari said, "Tell me about the place we're going to today."

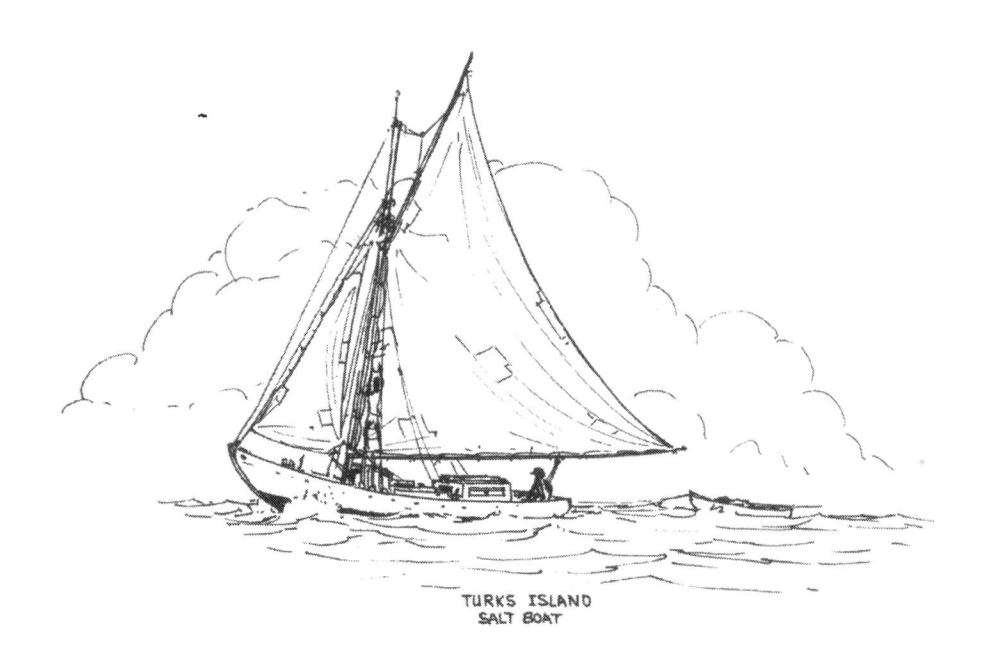

TURKS ISLAND
SALT BOAT

EL CARISAL

In the morning, Shari went into town to do some last-minute shopping, leaving Neil at the Cuernavaca house to arrange for a car for their trip to the coast. They left Cuernavaca at noon and drove the highway south across two mountain ranges, past the nearly dry, rock-strewn Rio Balsa.

At Acapulco, they skirted the city and drove north along the coastal road until they reached a small fishing village. There they stopped to buy bread, cheese, and a bottle of Pulque. Neil handed the bottle to Shari. "For our night-time pleasures," he said and added, "The downfall of a God, Ce Acatl's weakness."

"What?" Shari asked, as she held the bottle to the light to see the worm-like larva in the bottom.

"I told you about that when we visited Tepozteco," Neil said with a laugh. "Ce Acatl had another weakness that I'll demonstrate for you tonight. I think you'll like El Carisal," he said as they drove on. "It's a lot like the Bahamas, except for the Pacific surf pounding the shore. For dinner, the owners of the place cook fish for their guests on an open fire. At night you can hear the changing tide by the sound of the surf." Neil paused and added, "It's a perfect place to be alone together for a while before John arrives."

Johnny Boeuf was expected to fly in the next week. Neil and Shari planned to meet him at the Acapulco airport.

"That's just what we need," Shari enthused. "Someplace at sea-level, away from the mountains and at peace by the sea. Thank God!"

Neil drove on looking ahead at the road. His thoughts were of the night before and how Shari's body merged with his when they made love.

At the entrance to El Carisal, there is a single gatepost topped by a wooden bird with outstretched wings. It has been there for many years with its black wings spread out under sun and rain. Whenever Neil visited El Carisal, he felt compelled to stop and look at it.

"What's the significance of the bird?" Shari asked when they were at the gate. "Has it something to do with El Carisal?" she inquired while squinting up at the bird.

"No," Neil answered. "Carisal is a dwarf bamboo that grows around here."

Shari wasn't one to let a subject die so easily. "Then why the bird?" she asked.

With the cumulus clouds scudding above, it looked to Neil as if the bird was in flight. He looked away and shook his head as if to clear it. "It's just a decoration, a whim of Don Carlos, the owner," he said absently. Neil put the car in gear and drove across the earthen causeway that separated the sand dunes of El Carisal from the swamp and savannah to the east. He stopped behind a row of thatched huts and switched off the engine. "It's just a decoration," Neil reiterated, although Shari hadn't mentioned the bird again. "It's just a decoration," he repeated.

A man ran toward them from one of the huts. He was a powerfully built man for his age. Shari guessed he was seventy or older. His short cropped hair was white and there was a sparkle in his Castilian blue eyes. Don Carlos embraced Neil and kissed Shari's hand. As Neil made introductions, Don Carlos took in every detail of Shari, as if appraising a fine work of art.

When Don Carlos walked the lovers to their hut, he held Shari's hand the whole way. Neil was amused by his friend's blatant approval of Shari. He was sure she was enjoying the attention. The huts were all alike, crudely built of concrete blocks with conical thatched roofs. At the apex of each roof, a clay pot was inverted over the protruding center pole. Inside, there was a straw mattress, a naked light bulb, a fan, and a shower stall and toilet. Outside and not twenty yards away, Pacific surf pounded an endless deserted beach. It was the off season and Neil and Shari were Don Carlos' only guests.

"It has been long since I have seen you, my friend." Don Carlos emphasized as he embraced Neil once more. Then, he turned to observe Shari's legs as she bent to feel the mattress. He turned back to Neil. "Where have you taken yourself since our last times together?" he asked.

"Vivo en Las Bahamas." Neil replied.

Don Carlos' face lit up in recognition. "Aha! En Las Islas Baha Mar," he said, using the archaic Spanish name for the

Bahama Islands. "Is it as beautiful there as our El Carisal?" he asked.

"A different kind of beautiful." Neil replied.

"Aye! Una hermosa diferente!" Don Carlos repeated absently. He was too preoccupied watching Shari to think of islands or any other beauty.

Neil put both hands on Don Carlos 'shoulders. "My friend," he said smiling broadly. "I see you still have an eye for the ladies. You should be ashamed. You are a father of six!"

Don Carlos roared with laughter, took his eyes off Shari, and turned to Neil. "Eleven children," he said. "And two of them are girls!" He held up two fingers. "And recently I am the father of a son by an Indian from the hills." He paused with a serious expression and looked into Neil's eyes. "You have been away much too long, amigo," he said. "Much has happened in our years apart. Don Rojas is causing trouble with his gang of cut throats."

Neil didn't want to hear about politics. So, he changed the subject. "So, you have a new young wife, eh?" Neil said, trying to recall the words of a Gaucho ballad. "A young wife and many children are all an old man needs for a good life." Neil wasn't sure he remembered it correctly.

Don Carlos broke into laughter again. "There are now two young wives," he corrected and chuckled at Neil's surprise. "I have taken a second wife from Culebra Pueblo," he said proudly. "And she has given me two fine sons."

After Don Carlos left, Neil drove the car close in behind the hut and unloaded the trunk. It seemed they were well-prepared for the trek through the jungle to find John's crazy friend. Neil planned for them to live off the land. There would be sufficient water in the streams and rivers. He had purification tablets for that. Shari had her crossbow for hunting. Their Indian guides would bring their rifles to hunt game along the way. There were tapirs, monkeys, an occasional wild goat, and there was fruit and tubers in the jungle. So food would be no problem.

Back in Nassau, John had explained where he thought his friend lived. What concerned Neil was the fact that the man was insane. They were going in search of a mad man in one of the most remote and unexplored areas in Central America. Neil had warned

John that the trip would be extremely difficult and dangerous. However, John would not be discouraged. "Schildkroten is worth any effort," he insisted and added reassuringly, "Neil, you will understand when you meet him." With his natural curiosity and Shari's enthusiasm for the journey, Neil agreed to lead the expedition.

On a clear day, looking inland from El Carisal, the dark mass of El Culebra Volcano looms above the coastal swamps and savannah. El Culebra is dormant and has been since recorded time. It is the focus of legend and superstition, some of it dating to before the Spanish conquest.

"Why is it called Culebra?" Shari asked.

"Culebra is 'snake 'in Spanish, as you know," Neil replied. "My guess is it's a local Indian name. Don Carlos thinks it's named because it lets out smoke that curls up into the sky like a snake. That's the best explanation I've heard."

BONEFISHING

DON CARLOS
The Party

The last night at El Carisal, they ate mackerel cooked on the beach over an open fire by Don Carlos' wives. It was a festive occasion with the host's many children, grandchildren, friends, and relatives. Carlos presided over the party from a hammock with a guitar on his lap and a bottle of his favorite wine. Children were everywhere, running in and out of the firelight, and shouting in the Mestizo language. It was difficult for Neil to tell the children from the grandchildren.

Shari sat with the women, practicing her Spanish and learning the local dialect from Don Carlos' wives. As the evening progressed, there was music and singing while the guests drank wine and pulque. Someone chanted a tango love song in counterpoint to a guitar.

"I didn't love her when we met. Then one day she said firmly, 'I'm tired of everything' and she left. It was then I fell in love. I sacrificed so much trying to forget her. I wasted my life in bars telling everyone I forgot her. It was a lie!"

Late at night, with everyone asleep in their hammocks, the fire died out. Only Neil and Shari remained awake. Don Carlos was asleep in his hammock with a grandchild by his side. Shari covered them with a rebozo. Then, she and Neil walked back to their hut.

For a while, they lay awake listening to the surf and laughing at the mice playing in the thatched roof. Soon, laughter turned to lust and they made love on the straw mattress.

As Neil drifted off to sleep, he heard Shari say, "I've never seen a man so content with life and so at peace with the world." He knew she meant Don Carlos.

Neil awoke beside Shari and they made love in the darkness. When she fell back asleep, he lay awake listening to the mice. Then, he arose and went down onto the moonlit beach. A warm wind was blowing in from the sea. To the north, El Culebra's massive silhouette dominated the night sky.

When Neil returned to the hut, Shari lay naked on the mattress with her hands behind her head. Her sun-tanned body was silhouetted in the moonlit darkness and her shaven delta glowed temptingly. She spread her legs, one knee askew, as if challenging Neil to pleasure her. And he did.

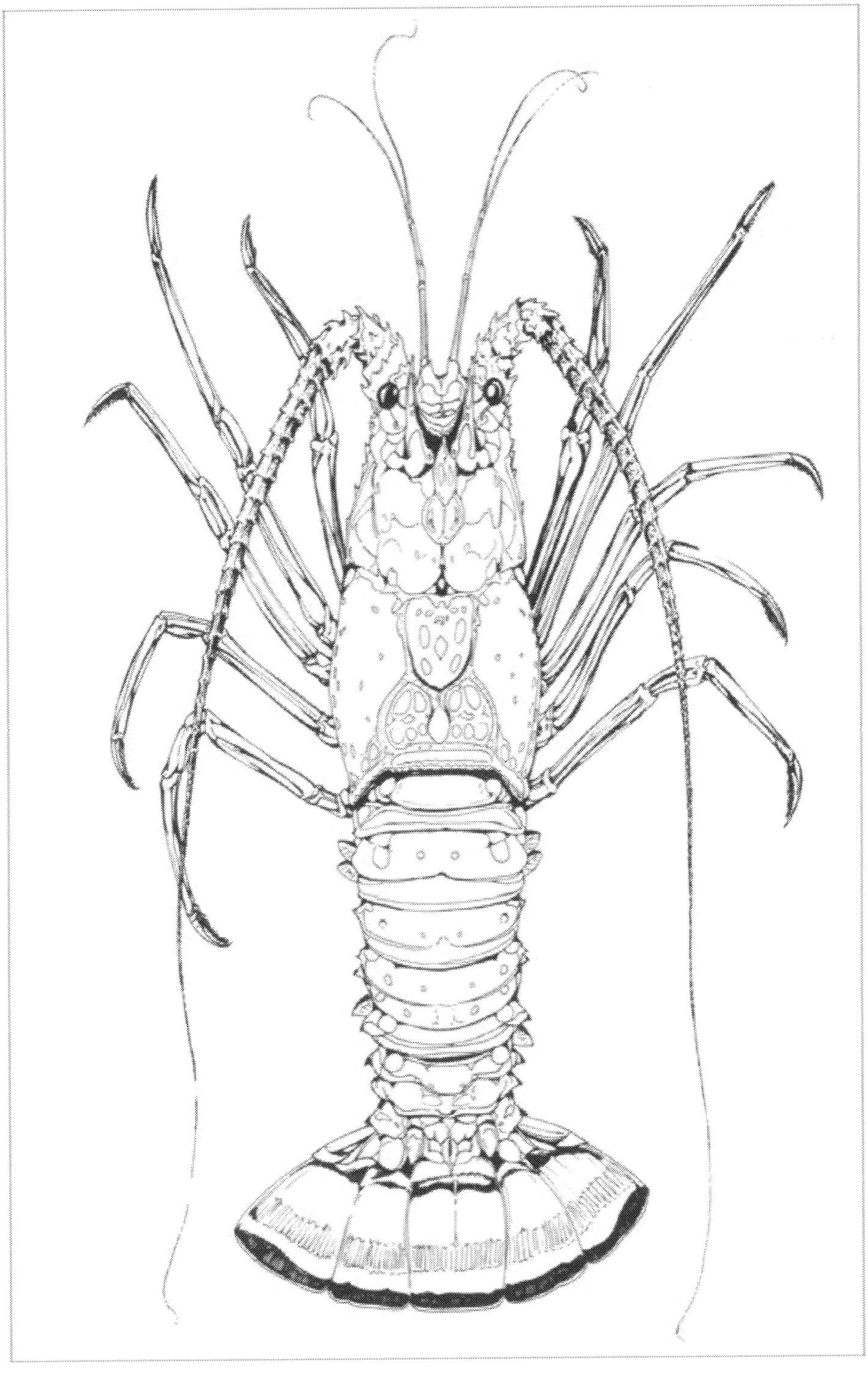

BAHAMA ENTRY

Here I want to tell how easy it was to go through customs and immigration in the days before the Out Islands were called Family Islands. Whenever I entered the Bahamas at Nassau, I raised the yellow Q flag and anchored Island Girl off the eastern end of Prince George Wharf, where the customs and immigration offices were located. An officer would come out in one of the glass-bottom charter boats and clear me in.

The formalities were brief and simple. "What's your citizenship?" One wasn't often asked to prove it. "Do you have any fruit, vegetables, animals, or firearms aboard?" That was the extent of it. I would sign a paper and the officer would give me a Transire document allowing Island Girl to cruise the Bahamas. We would shake hands, and that was it.

After a number of entries, I became acquainted with the officials. They knew me and my vessel. One officer in particular was quite friendly and helpful. Perhaps it was because we shared the surname Johnson. It became so that only Officer Johnson did the formalities when I entered port. The problem was, he suffered from mal-de-mer, and the ride out and back in a glass-bottom boat was agony for him.

Officer Johnson never set foot aboard Island Girl. He would ask the required questions and give me a paper to sign along with the Transire. Then he would rush back ashore.

On one occasion, I entered after a rough crossing from Key West with my cat, Grommet, and a litter of new-born kittens. When Officer Johnson came out to clear me in, he quickly asked the usual questions and without waiting for a reply, he gave me the Transire and signed the entry form himself. As I lowered the quarantine flag, I noticed the bag of oranges hanging in the rigging, my rifle in its rack in the cabin, and I heard Grommet's kittens meowing for their mother. Things were so simple and easy in those days.

NASSAU DINGHY

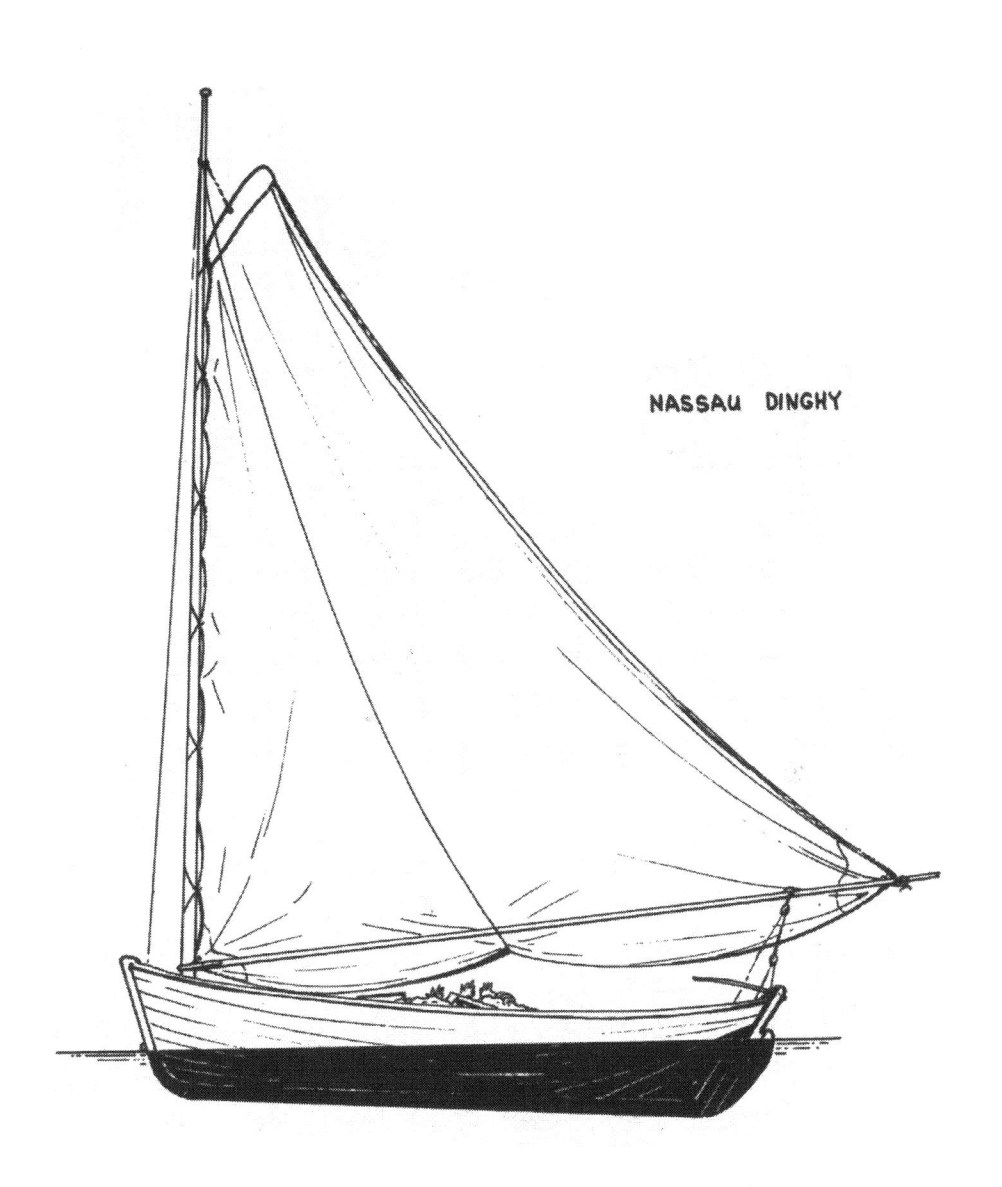

EPILOGUE

In my younger days, I said that when I die, it should be at sea, under sail, and in the arms of a beautiful woman. That dream will never come to pass. I'm content to go now with Frenchie, my loving cat beside me.

I do not fear death. I have died before and I will die again. Perhaps, I'll come back as a roach in Australia or a stray dog in Abaco. Who knows but God?

I felt that I could not live another day without Frenchie, but now my world has changed, and with Rachael in my life I want to live forever. Look back, not in sadness, but with a smile.

REMEMBER NOW

It is night and we sit on the porch sipping wine, talking, laughing, and looking into the eyes of our friends. The tide changes and the surf breaks on Tilloo. There's a high wind in the trees and dogs are barking in the distance. Frogs croak and out in the bush, a rooster crows.

In time all this will change. It will alter or simply go away. We will change and tomorrow will never be as today.

When we and our friends are gone and when dogs no longer bark, the surf will still break on Tilloo. Somewhere in the bush, a cock will crow. The moon and sun will rise and set, and the wind will caress the trees as our memories are washed away by time.

So we must remember Now!

SHORT SNORTER

During WWII, soldiers, mainly airmen, collected paper money from countries they visited. Beginning with a U.S. dollar, the bills were taped together end-to-end and kept in rolls. Wherever a man went, he added on bills and had his friends and acquaintances sign them.

Those rolls of exotic currency were known as "Short Snorters." When a group of airmen got together, usually at a bar, they rolled out their short snorters and compared them to see who had the longest and the most signatures. The winner earned free drinks.

My cousin Charles, a fighter pilot in the Army Air Corps told me that some rolls were over twenty feet long. As a boy of ten, I had to have a short snorter of my own. So I collected bills, made a roll, and had everyone I knew sign it. My short snorter was well short of twenty feet for sure, but I was proud of it.

I believe the term "Snorter" refers to a drink like a snort of rum!

PAUL & THE STRANGER'S SONG

"Where were you before you went to live with your grandfather?" Don asked.

"Astride the Tropic of Cancer on a small island," Paul replied, "With my mother and my childhood friends." He paused for a moment reflecting. "I have good memories of those years before she died. That was when I went to my grandfather's island."

John was listening nearby with a third drink in hand. "Hey, Paul!" he interrupted. "What's your most vivid memory of childhood? Is it tactile, visual, or auditory?"

"Oh boy!" Don groaned remembering John's obsession with details.

Paul smiled at his friend John, the imbiber, the defrocked priest.

"I would say that, what impressed me most…" Paul said thoughtfully. "Was something auditory. It was a song I heard when I was seven."

John moved in closer. "Tell me. Was it an island song, a classic piece, or a ballad?"

"A ballad I suppose," Paul answered. "I heard the song once and not again for many years. Each time I heard it, it touched my soul in a different way."

As his friends listened, Paul told of a stranger who came to his island one stormy night and sang a song that changed his life.

"I was living with my mother then," Paul continued. "She and the people of the island were my family and my only influence. We were isolated there from the world. A mail boat came once a month and there was no airstrip. The people lived by subsistence farming and fishing. We ate chicken, fish, okra, corn, pigeon peas, and rice. We children picked dillies and guavas from the trees and coco-plums on the dunes. We dug turtle eggs on the beach and gathered dove eggs in the bush. There was no chewing gum. So, we chewed sap from the dilly trees. It was a hard life for the grown-ups, but a full and happy one for us kids. We lived close to nature and our imaginations were stirred by the folk tales of the elders. Mine was a magical childhood."

"What about your father?" Don asked. "You haven't mentioned him."

"I never knew my father. He was lost at sea before I was born. Every family on the island had lost someone at sea and many of my friends were fatherless. It was a fact of life that we lived with and accepted."

John broke in. "What about the song?" He asked impatiently.

"Okay!" Paul said. "But first I want to set the scene."

"The only social life on the island was a weekly family get-together at a bar adjacent to the mail boat dock. Those get-togethers were a chance for families to socialize, tell stories, and sing hymns while we children played outside. When it grew late, we would come inside and listen to the stories the elders told with gestures and rhythmic chanting. I would lay on my mother's lap, listening to the stories and then drift off to sleep. I looked forward to those weekly meetings," Paul said with a waning smile. "There was peace and serenity there." He paused and shook his head, "I have never known such peace."

"Go on," Don prompted. "Tell us about the song."

"It was on a stormy, moonless night that I first heard the song. Rain squalls had set in at sunset. The wind was at full gale and everyone was gathered in the bar. Rain was pelting the roof. The shutters were rattling and banging. We children were inside for a change, and there was a pungent odour from the kerosene lamps. Mr. Cooper, the schoolmaster, was strumming a guitar, but it couldn't be heard over the pounding rain and howling wind. It was the sort of night when one is thankful to be safe and dry inside."

Paul glanced at his friends and continued, "Even as a child I was thankful for safety and warmth on such a night.

"Suddenly a man ran in, saying the mail boat had come in from the storm. The crew and passengers were on their way to the bar. The Captain and crew of the mail boat were known by everyone, but their passenger, a young white man, was not. He was a stranger. There were greetings and talk of the weather. Food and drinks were passed around.

"The stranger borrowed Mr. Cooper's guitar, strummed it expertly and tuned it. Even to my untrained ears, it sounded better. Then the man stood at the bar and sang a song that none of us had ever heard. It told of love, loss, and nostalgia. It affected everyone in the room. Even at my young age it touched my heart. No one spoke while the stranger sang and all eyes were upon him. The beating rain and howling wind seemed to accompany the man as he played and sang. Everyone was lost in thought; in esoteric memory. It was that kind of a song."

Paul paused. "I was deeply moved," he said. "I had no idea why. Years later," Paul continued, "as an adult, and far from the Islands, I heard the song again and it took on meaning for me. It brought back childhood memories of peace and comfort, and newer things that I was unaware of as a child. I had matured, experienced life, and known love and loss."

Paul wiped his eyes with the back of his hand. "Now, whenever I hear that song, I remember the night a stranger came to our island and sang to us."

"What was the song?" John asked impatiently, but Paul would.

THE CONSTRUCTION SHED

When I turn from my drawing board and look at the wall behind me, the painting is there. I gaze at it from my bed and it reminds me of the thoughtfulness of another and of my youth.

My father studied the Italian Renaissance painters and learned the formulas of the paints they used. He duplicated their formulas and mixed his own colours.

He spent two years indoors, painting still-lifes. Then in the spring of 1947, Pops went outdoors to paint. He did an oil on canvas of a construction shed behind our home.

I was 15 at the time, involved with a girlfriend, and looking forward to my 16th birthday. When Pops finished the painting, he framed it and gave it to his friend and architecture partner, Marion Wyeth.

Fifty-five years later, I was living on a small island in the Northern Bahamas, and Marion Wyeth's son, Buzzy learned of it. Buzzy and his sisters, Florance, Alice, and Joanie were older than me. They ran with a different crowd. So, I never really knew them.

I hadn't seen Buzzy since 1940, but he must have remembered me, because one day a friend from a neighbouring island brought me a package from a Marion Wyeth, Jr. It was my father's painting of the construction shed! There was no note, just the carefully-wrapped painting.

What wonderful memories that painting brings to me now, hanging here on the wall! I remember the taste of Surinam cherries from the tree behind Pop's office, the odour of his pipe tobacco, the scent of patchouli perfume, and the nostalgia of my first romance. Most of all I'm reminded of the thoughtfulness and generosity of someone I barely knew.

2015: My dad kept in touch with Alice Wyeth and her husband Henry Barkhausen until he died. After that, I received a Christmas card from Alice and Henry each year. Henry and I had a lot in common. He was a boat builder and an avid sailor. He built several 35-foot gaff-rigged sloops, none with engines, and a miniature tug boat to tow them when needed. He built the tug in his basement. To get it out, they had to excavate and breach the foundations.

In 2012 at the age of 97, Henry laid the keel of another vessel. Being a realist, he named it "Final Effort," and by December 2015 she was completed and Henry had turned 100!

FREEMAN McKENZIE'S BAHAMA SLOOP

LOVE POTION

Lord Garn was an elderly bachelor who owned a vast estate on Windermere Island, Eleuthera.

One Spring, he arrived on the island with a beautiful wife, thirty years his junior. Lord Garn was in his seventies then, and because of the disparity in age with his wife, he began taking daily doses of an aphrodisiac bush medicine known as boar hog bush. It was supplied by his gardener. Evidently it worked, because the newlyweds spent a happy and satisfying summer on the Island.

When ready to return to England, Lord Garn persuaded the gardener to give him dried boar hog bush to take back. The gardener cautioned his employer to use it in moderation and only in the amount he had been taking while on the island.

The happy couple departed for the UK, and a month later Lord Garn was dead.

Note: It is said that the Dodder or Love Vine, which is poison, is also an aphrodisiac.

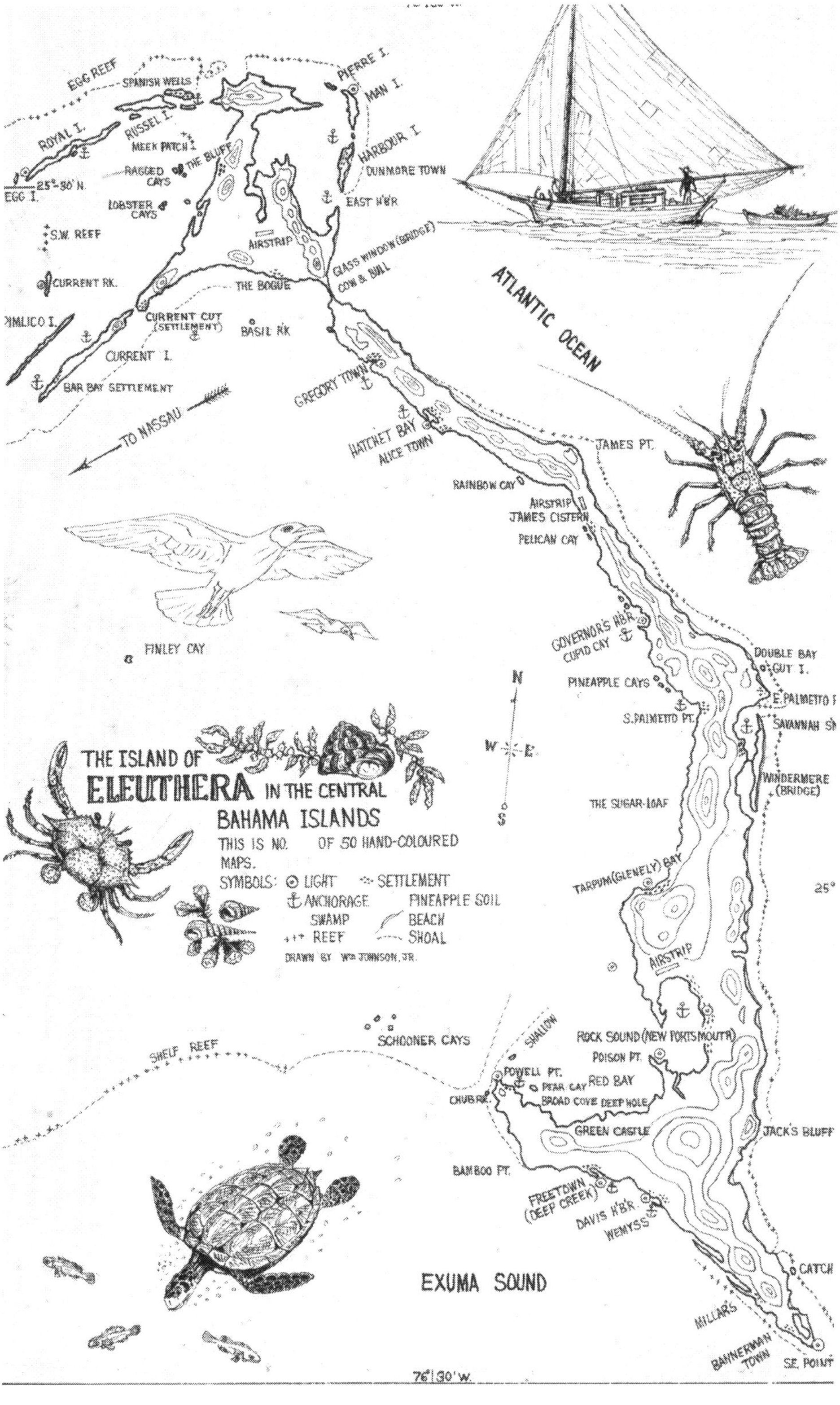
THE ISLAND OF
ELEUTHERA IN THE CENTRAL
BAHAMA ISLANDS
THIS IS NO. OF 50 HAND-COLOURED MAPS.
SYMBOLS: LIGHT SETTLEMENT
ANCHORAGE PINEAPPLE SOIL
SWAMP BEACH
REEF SHOAL
DRAWN BY Wm JOHNSON, JR.
ATLANTIC OCEAN
EXUMA SOUND
EGG REEF
SPANISH WELLS
ROYAL I.
RUSSEL I.
MEEK PATCH
THE BLUFF
RAGGED CAYS
EGG I.
25°-30' N.
LOBSTER CAYS
S.W. REEF
CURRENT RK.
PIMLICO I.
CURRENT CUT (SETTLEMENT)
CURRENT I.
BAR BAY SETTLEMENT
TO NASSAU
PIERRE I.
MAN I.
HARBOUR I.
DUNMORE TOWN
EAST H'B'R
AIRSTRIP
GLASS WINDOW (BRIDGE)
COW & BULL
THE BOGUE
BASIL RK
GREGORY TOWN
HATCHET BAY
ALICE TOWN
JAMES PT.
RAINBOW CAY
AIRSTRIP
JAMES CISTERN
PELICAN CAY
GOVERNOR'S H'B'R
CUPID CAY
FINLEY CAY
DOUBLE BAY
GUT I.
PINEAPPLE CAYS
S. PALMETTO PT.
E. PALMETTO
SAVANNAH
WINDERMERE (BRIDGE)
THE SUGAR-LOAF
TARPUM (GLENELY) BAY
25°
AIRSTRIP
SCHOONER CAYS
SHALLOW
SHELF REEF
ROCK SOUND (NEW PORTSMOUTH)
POISON PT.
POWELL PT.
PEAR CAY
RED BAY
BROAD COVE
DEEP HOLE
GREEN CASTLE
JACK'S BLUFF
BAMBOO PT.
FREETOWN (DEEP CREEK)
DAVIS H'B'R.
WEMYSS
CATCH
MILLARS
BANNERMAN TOWN
SE. POINT
76° 30' W.
N
W
E
S

FRIEZE AU VENT

During my time at the nightclub in Nassau, I met a Polish/Frenchman named Romaine. He had been an officer in the Free Polish Navy during the war and was made a French citizen. He later moved to Casablanca and married a Berber woman. After a few years, he realized his marriage was floundering. Being afraid of repercussions from his wealthy and influential in-laws, he set about building a boat.

When the vessel was completed, he christened it "Frieze au Vent" and sailed away.

Months later, Romaine landed in Martinique. He continued sailing north through the Windward and Leeward Islands where he found work. After a year there, he sailed north through the islands and ended up sun blind in Turks and Caicos. The crawfish company there took him in and nursed him back to health. To repay them, Romaine worked a year for the company.

When I met him, he had recently arrived in Nassau from Turks and Caicos. That winter, we collaborated on artwork for the bar at the Buena Vista Hotel. Romaine was addicted to available women and he frequented the Paradise Bordello, a local whore house. It seems he had frequented every whore house on his route from Martinique to Nassau.

Aboard "Frieze au Vent," there was an Amazon parrot he stole from a bordello in the Dominican Republic. The bird shrieked obscenities in three languages and kept whore-house hours by sleeping until noon each day.

After the job at Buena Vista was done, I was commissioned to do an exploration survey of Great Harbour Cay in the Berry Islands. Romaine wanted to sail there in company with me, but there was one problem. "Frieze au Vent," though only 18 feet in length, drew three feet nine inches. "Island Girl" drew only three six. Forgetting this, I led Romaine over the banks from Bonds Cay to Bullocks Harbour. As Island Girl's worm shoe would be scraping sand, Frise au Vent would be hard aground astern.

With the help of a full moon tide, we finally reached Bullocks Harbour, and I began the survey. At that time there were a dozen families in the settlement of Bullocks Harbour. It was the only settlement on the large island of Great Harbour Cay. The men made a living crawfishing, while the women tended small subsistence farms.

At dawn each day, a dozen sailing dinghies would set out for Russell Shoals, and at sunset they would return loaded with crawfish. The crawfish were kept in a floating cage, anchored in the harbour. Once a month, a motor vessel came from Nassau to pick them up. Aside from a single radio locked onto ZNS, the government station, that monthly boat was the settlement peoples' only contact with the outside world.

During the survey, I came across two mockingbirds eating fermented palmetto berries. They were too drunk to fly. So, they staggered off into the bushes.

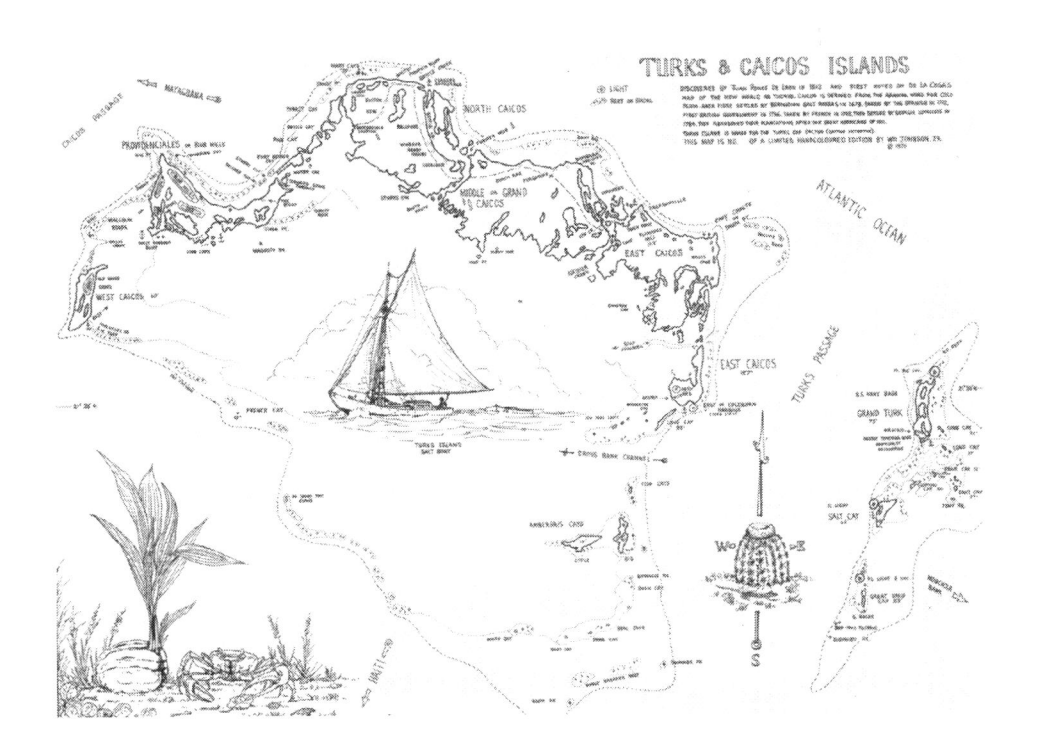

WRECKS

On the dunes of the two-mile ocean beach, there was a sign marking a path to Bullocks Harbour settlement. It read in crudely painted letters, 'Wrecks.' I was told it was put there to help castaways find their way to safety.

I also Solved the mystery of the waterfall I had heard about. It turned out to be a rock ledge over which the tide flowed into a lagoon.

When the survey was completed and we were ready to return to Nassau, Romaine said that, being a blue-water sailor, he would take the ocean route back.

A week later we were anchored side by side in the lee of Potters Cay. Romaine was a rational and well-educated man, but he admitted to what he called a material obsession.

On his Atlantic crossing, as "Frieze au Vent" sailed under twin headsails, he would listen to the sea rushing by, and after a few weeks he began imagining it was wearing a groove in the waterline.

He knew that was impossible, but nevertheless he would reach down and feel the waterline. Being alone at sea for months on end does strange things to the human mind.

Some years later, Romaine married an American woman, bought Tom Waddington's schooner "Olad," and sailed off to the Mediterranean.

A DRUNKEN SAILOR

My friend, Gerald was the caretaker at Lyford Cay long before it was developed. His home was a stuffy, rat-infested thatched hut. So, he spent most of his time aboard his little smack boat.

Gerald was a heavy drinker, and he would disappear for weeks on end. I often encountered him in distant harbours or under sail, far out at sea. Gerald was a loner and an erratic wanderer.

I remember during a particularly clear, cool winter night with the stars and planets seemingly within reach, there was buttonwood smoke in the air from the cook fires of the fishing fleet. (For me, that odour, mixed with the stench of rotting fish, is the essence of the old Nassau market wharf.) Out in the harbour, Gerald's smack boat was drifting on the ebb tide. Its mainsail was set and Gerald was passed out over the tiller, chanting a litany, "I'm Gerald, Fitzgerald, king of the sea and master of none!"

I wasn't worried. I had seen him that way before. The tide would carry him out to sea where he would sober up under the morning sun and sail home in the afternoon.

Aye, those were Halcyon days! They were days of rum and laughter, of good friends and worthy lovers.

How long ago did we run barefoot through the streets of old Nassau town? All that remains now are memories. There are no more pixies in the palm trees or mermaids in the sea.

I'll surely remember them, but will they remember me?

COOPERJACK CAY

When I look east from my home on Lubbers Quarters, I see Cooperjack Cay sheltered in the lee of Tilloo. The locals call it "Cubbiejack."

There must be a story behind the name of that little island. In the olden days, Cooperjacks were the barrel-makers on whaling ships. Perhaps a shipwrecked cooperjack once lived on the island.

Today Cooperjack Cay is privately owned and my Haitian friend Jerry is the caretaker.

I have inquired, but no one seems to know the island's history.

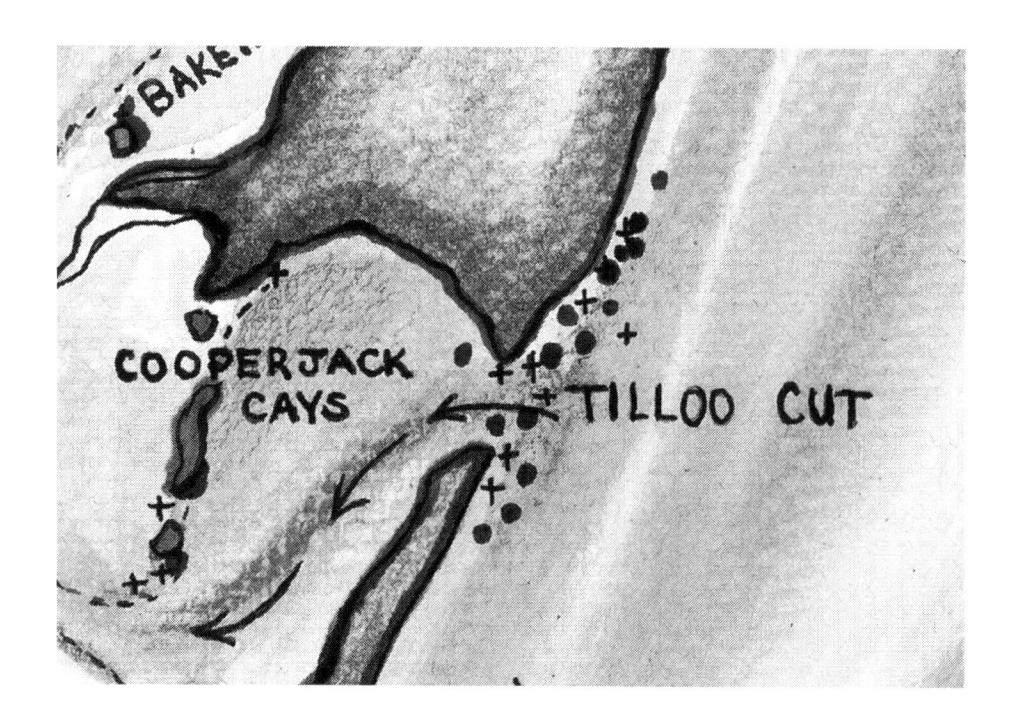

ELENA'S TOMB

It was a time of cholera and the American doctor in Key West was in love with Elena, the nineteen-year-old daughter of a prominent family. Of course, they disapproved and made every effort to keep the two apart.

At twenty, Elena died and her body was entombed in a marble vault. The doctor went mad with grief and moved into a shack on the beach. Some time later it was found that the tomb had been broken open, and Elena's body was missing. When the police finally found the doctor, he was living with her body.

JAPAN JAUNITO

In March, when the cherry trees were in bloom, I earned an Ichidan in Judo. I studied Buddhist philosophy and I practiced Zen meditation until I could reach the alpha state. My goal was to achieve Satori. How foolish I was!

Between the disciplines of Judo and my studies of Buddhism, I found pleasure in the arms of Aiko and her friend Michiko. I studied Shibari under Michiko, an experienced practitioner of the art. We used it in our astral projection experiments along with other forms of sensory deprivations such as blindfolding and isolation. Our experiments were primitive and inconclusive, but they set me on a path to Satori.

I walked that path for many years, and now, because of Juanito, I have ceased the quest. Juanito believed he could avoid death, and he may have succeeded, because we remember him now.

Juanito spent many years seeking the ideal of every one of the human senses in the hope of finding perfection and enlightenment. He studied the world's religions and steeped himself in the disciplines of mind and body until he believed he had everything in proper order. At that point he set out to achieve what no man had, to deny mortality and cheat the grim reaper.

Last week we buried Juanito at Punta Arenas.

ED SHEEDY, TOKYO

Ed Sheedy was a family friend who was older than me by thirty years. He was tall and handsome in the mold of Errol Flynn, whom he somewhat resembled. Ed was independently wealthy, and as far as I know, he never had a job. He had been married and divorced three times and wasn't about to make those mistakes again. Ed was a good-natured tippler with an addiction to younger women, and he played the field with gentlemanly gusto! Whenever I saw Ed, he was with a lovely woman.

As an adult, I was living in Tokyo and training at the Kodokan for a black belt in judo. When I walked home in the evening, I had to go through the red-light district. That is where a chance encounter occurred.

As I walked past a Joy House, the door opened with a burst of light and music, and out stepped Ed Sheedy with a whore on each arm. Although drunk, he recognized me right away. "Bill!" he shouted. "What in hell are you doing here?" I hesitated to ask the same question. As we stood talking on the crowded sidewalk, I sensed Ed's embarrassment. We handled the situation well, and after a while we shook hands and parted.

On my return to America, I ran into Ed having dinner with a beautiful young woman. I saw his apprehension at seeing me again. No mention was made of our Tokyo encounter.

THE HOUSE OF DAWN
Excerpt from Esperanza

It was eight o'clock on a Sunday morning in Santiago, Cuba. Johnny Boeuf and Juanito were drinking frozen Daiquiris in a seaside cantina, one like no other in the world, with a bordello on the floors above. The Cantina was affiliated with, and physically part of, the House of Dawn, the most popular and most notorious whore house in Oriente Province.

"Do you have a whore house like this in your Bahama Islands?" Juanito asked, squinting out the doorway into sunlight reflecting off the harbour waters.

Johnny sipped his drink thoughtfully. "Nothing as elaborate as what is upstairs here," he replied. "Not with such a variety of women. Our house in Nassau is a small business with only three whores, and it's not a place to stay overnight. It's a true whore house, not a bordello."

"Only three putas to serve your whole island?" Juanito was mystified. "They must be always tired from the sex."

John explained that prostitution was against the law in the Bahamas, and that it had to be kept low-key. Juanito shook his head in disbelief. "Que antiquado!" he said.

"I'm afraid so!" John admitted. "Our British Colonial laws are old-fashioned and out of date. Our abogados still bill their clients in Guineas instead of pounds and shillings."

Juanito had no idea what a Guinea was and he was too drunk to ask. The two men sat in thought, listening to the sounds of the town coming awake outside.

John had come from the mountains two days before to meet Juanito at the House of Dawn. It was their safe house in Santiago, a place out of sight of Batista's federal police. Ironically, the establishment was frequented by the Alcalde of Santiago, the police chief, and most local government officials. Yet, it was a refuge for revolutionaries like John and Juanito.

Juanito broke the contemplative silence. "My friend," he said, "I observe that you situate yourself with your back to the wall or in a corner when we are in a public place. You are seated in such a way now. Why is it you do so?"

"I like to watch the entrance to see who comes and goes." John explained. Then he added, "I suppose it's conditioned paranoia."

"Survival!" Juanito exclaimed, and having no idea what John had just said, he quickly changed the subject.

"I have never been to your Nassau. Is it similar to Santiago?"

"It's very beautiful, but vastly different," John answered. "The town isn't as old or as picturesque as your Santiago. There is not the profusion of wrought iron and decorative stucco as here. We also have no mountains," he added.

John could see that Juanito was interested. So, he continued, "Oddly enough, there's a connection between Santiago and the Bahama Islands. Back in the 1800s, the artist Winslow Homer painted watercolour pictures in both places. On his visit to Santiago, he had an affair with the wife of the Alcalde and he was run out of town and off the island. There is an unfinished painting of the unfaithful woman standing on a balcony behind a wrought iron railing, dressed in a mantilla and shawl."

Juanito smiled at the mention of a mantilla. "The mantilla is an antique tradition," he said. "It is like the matrimonial bed sheet displayed on a balcony the morning after a wedding. Sadly, there are none of those traditions alive today."

It was John's turn to be mystified. "What's that about? 'A bed sheet?'" he asked.

Juanito grinned. "In past times, it was tradition that a woman remain a virgin until marriage. To prove it, the matrimonial bed sheet was hung on the balcony the morning after a wedding for all to see."

John was puzzled. "How did that prove her virginity?"

"If there was blood on the sheet, that was the proof," Juanito laughed and added, "It is said that many a bride pricked her finger on her wedding night!"

John laughed, "Human nature. It's universal, spanning time and culture. It has no limits."

"You, my friend, are un filosofo!" Juanito said with undisguised admiration.

The cantina was becoming crowded as men wandered in from the rooms above. When three unfamiliar faces appeared, John and Juanito rose and walked out onto the harbour road.

In the early sunlight, the fishing smacks were unloading their catch from a night offshore. The odour of fish was in the air. John was reminded of the market wharf in Nassau.

"Where is Esperanzo?" Juanito asked.

"En México, quisas," John replied in Spanish, thinking of the cold Daiquiris they had left un-drunk on the table in the cantina.

"I hope he is safe and with Shari again," said Juanito.

"I do not worry about Neil," John reassured. "He's a consummate survivor. Remember this my friend. Without hope, there is no survival."

SANTIAGO
Nostalgia

I remember Santiago as she was, with barrel-tile rooftops, verdant gardens and shaded verandas, and with high balconies overlooking the blue Caribbean. She was a city where wrought-iron shadows on a stucco wall evoked fantasies of times long past.

FOLDBOATS

One day while aboard Island Girl, I saw one of those Austrian canvas Foldboats heading my way. When it came alongside, a large sunburned man shipped his paddle and asked directions to the inland waterway. He was an Argentinian from a wealthy Buenos Aires family, and because he rebelled against President Peron, he had to leave the country.

Because the foldboat had no sail, he had paddled the entire distance from Buenos Aires, except for one leg of the journey, when he rode a freighter across the mouth of the Amazon River. The man was a health food advocate and he ate only natural foods. He subsisted on rain water and the fish he caught along the way.

That night we shared a meal aboard Island Girl, and in the morning, he paddled off to the inland waterway and I never saw nor heard of him again.

When I worked in a Nassau nightclub, a rather introverted middle-aged man used to come in for drinks each day. He told me he had cruised all the way from Maine in a sailing Foldboat, and that he intended circumnavigating the globe in it. We all thought he was crazy. Perhaps he was.

One night he announced he was continuing his journey the next day, and his first port of call would be Fresh Creek, Andros.

In the morning, a group of us gathered on Prince George Wharf to see the man off. We watched as he paddled away and sailed past Hog Island Light. We saw him slack sheets and run west toward the Tongue of the Ocean. It was the last we saw of him.

Some months later, the broken remains of the Foldboat were discovered on a sea-swept rock off Driggs Hill, Andros.

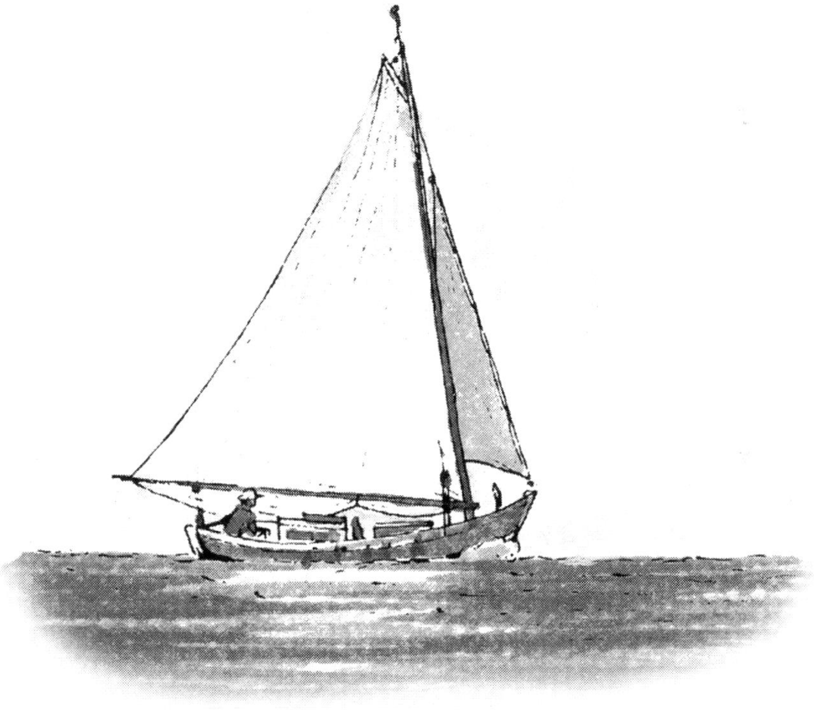

BOB WHITE IS MISSING

I knew Bob White as a competent seaman, a man who kept an orderly ship and took no chances. He made a living as a fishing guide and the captain of a 34-foot lapstrake wooden vessel with a gasoline engine. Bob was saving his money to buy a Diesel engine.

One summer day, Bob left Miami with two men for a week of fishing in the Bahamas. They crossed the Gulf Stream, cleared customs in Alice Town, and were last seen heading south along the edge of the Great Bahama Bank.

Bob had arranged with friends in Bimini to keep in touch by short-wave radio, but after a week with no word from him they began to worry. After ten days they reported him missing. The Miami Coast Guard sent out search planes and a cutter, but found nothing. (In those days there was no BASRA, Bahama Air Sea Rescue.)

After the Coast Guard gave up, Bob's friends and I searched every rock and cay as well as the waters from Bimini to Guinchos Cay, again with no results.

Bob's vessel was wood and it had a gasoline engine. So, if there had been a fire or explosion there would have been some debris. No sign of Bob White's boat was ever found. It was simply another mystery of the Bermuda Triangle.

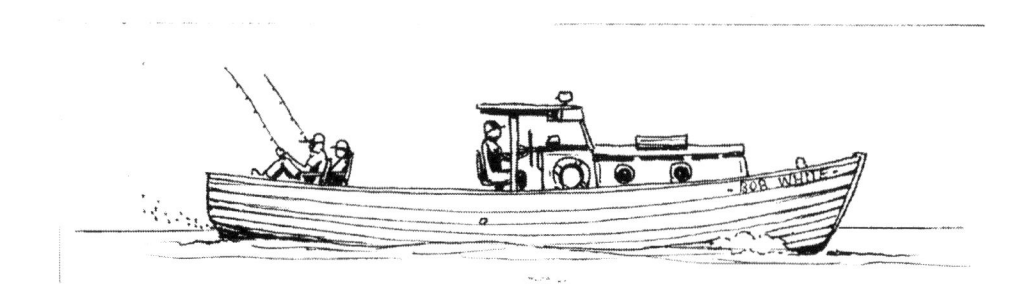

THE BERMUDA TRIANGLE

Bob White's little vessel is only one of many that have gone missing in the so-called Bermuda Triangle. Most notable are the Sulphur Queen, a large ship, and Harvey Conover's sailboat, Revnock.

There are many theories about the disappearances, from alien abduction to chemical changes in sea water. My friend John Gynell told me about an unexplained compass deviation he experienced on the bridge of a freighter. It was on an autopilot course from Cat Island to San Salvador.

It was a flat calm day and there was another freighter to port on a parallel course. Suddenly John's vessel began making a slow turn to port. He looked astern and saw his wake curving in an arc. The other freighter was making a similar turn. John checked the compass and it read the new course, although the autopilot was steering them as before. As he reached to disengage the autopilot, both vessels came back on course.

Another story of deviation was told by a friend flying from Crooked Island to Great Exuma. The weather was perfect and he was on VFR. On leaving Crooked Island, he put the plane on autopilot for George Town and began paying attention to his female passenger with an occasional glance out the window. When he estimated Great Exuma to be within sight, he looked out and saw only blue sea. No land was in sight where there should have been a chain of islands. He made a guess as to his position and altered course. Luckily, he guessed correctly, because when he landed at George Town airport, his fuel tanks were nearly empty.

Electronic anomalies affecting radios and GPS devices occur in several places in the Bahamas, notably around Lynyard Cay in the Abacos. Magnetic & GPS disturbance has been reported there by boats and Private aircraft and a number of fatal shipwrecks have occurred in the vicinity.

ANDROS BARE-HEAD

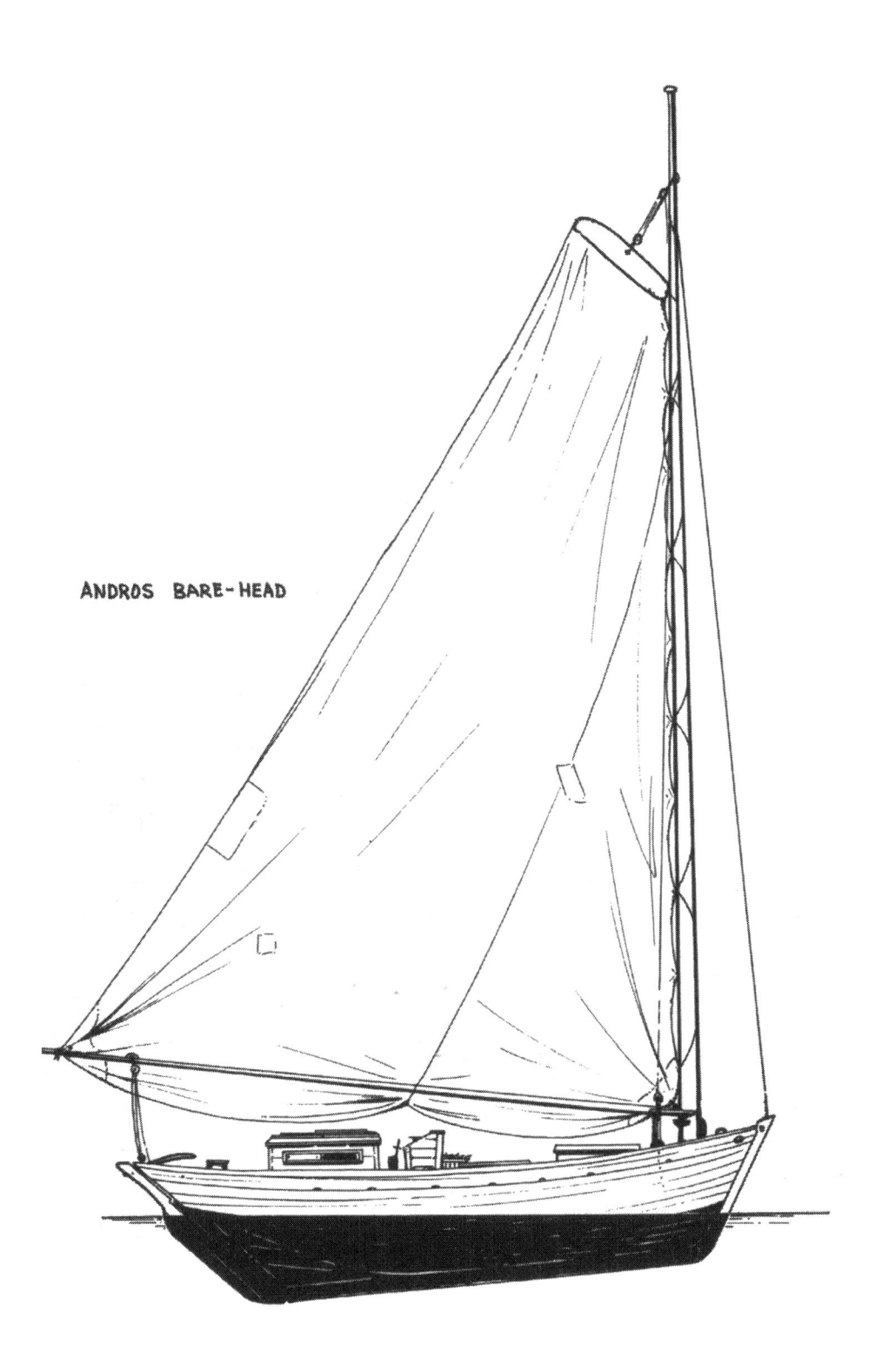

EXTINCT THEN FOUND

The West Indian Monk Seal and the Saltwater Crocodile are nearly extinct. (Note; there is a program to breed Saltwater Crocodiles in South Florida.) The dodo bird is gone forever from this earth along with the Auk (1850), the Passenger Pigeon (1914), the zebra-like Quagga (late 1800s), the Moa (early 1800s), the Lingula (Lantern Shell), the Balinese Tiger, and the Thylacine or Tasmanian Wolf.

However, there are two species of lizard-like reptiles, the Tuataras (*Sphenodon punctatus* and *S. guntheri*) that survive on a few small islands off the coast of New Zealand. They were thought to have become extinct some 200 million years ago during the Jurassic period. They grow to about two feet in length and resemble iguanas, but they are not true lizards. They belong to a separate order of reptiles and they have a vestigial pineal third eye.

In South Africa in 1938, the ichthyologist Dr J. L. B. Smith of Rhodes University discovered the Coelacanth, the lobe-finned fish (*Latimeria chalumnae*) living in the waters of the Indian Ocean. This living fossil was thought to have been extinct since the close of the Cretaceous period some 75 million years ago. Local native fishermen have been catching them for years. In the twentieth century, the Crinoid or "Sea Lilly" is a primitive form of Echinoderm from the Paleozoic era and was discovered in the depths of the ocean.

The European Tarpan horse (*Equus caballus gmelini*) became extinct before the Middle Ages due to hunting by humans, but in the mid 1800s, the Russian explorer Nikolay Mikhailovich Przhevalsky (also Przewalski) discovered a related and nearly extinct species of wild horse in Central Asia. The animal now bears his name, *Equus caballus Przewalski,* and it is no longer found in the wild.

In 1995, a French expedition in Tibet discovered a new species of wild horse in a hidden valley. DNA samples proved it to be a horse thought to be extinct.

In the plant kingdom, the Ginkgo Tree or Maidenhair Tree (*Ginkgo biloba*) would be extinct if not for the fact that it has been cultivated since ancient times in Chinese temple gardens. Recently, wild Ginkgo Trees were discovered in a hidden valley in Western China.

The genus Ginkgo is the sole representative of its family Ginkgoaceae, Order: Ginkgophyta Phylum: Ginkgophyta.

The insect, Mastotermes, has been extinct for 30 to 130 million years. But one species, *Mastotermes darwiniensis*, a link between cockroaches and termites, survives in Australia.

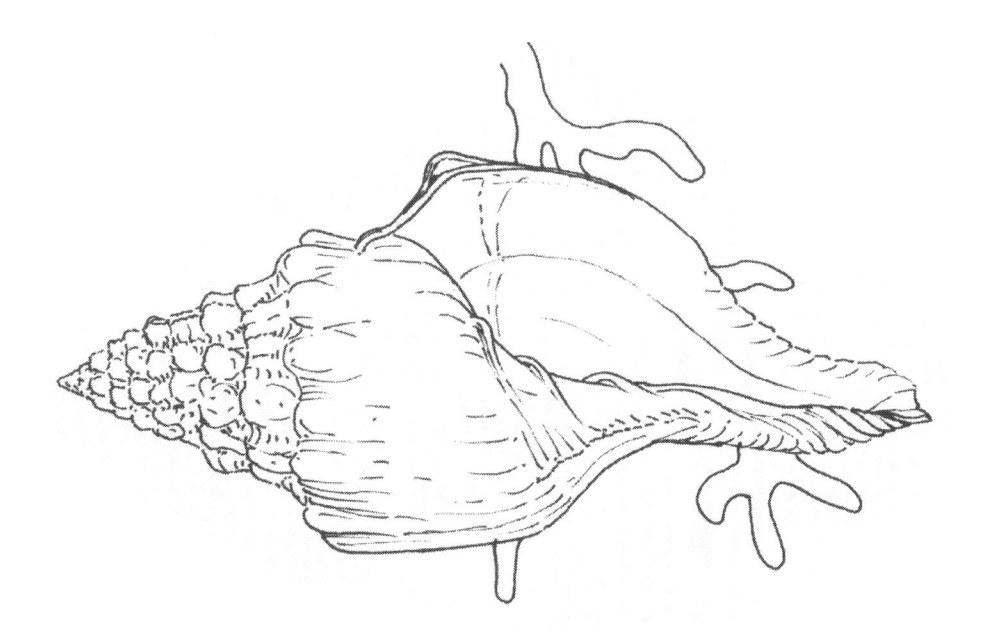

MOND & THE MERMAID
A Children's Story

Mond, as a boy of eight, worked with his uncle Willie on a small farm cultivating corn, okra, and pigeon peas. They also grew melons. Mond lived with his family in the settlement of Red Bays on Andros Island in the Bahamas.

To the east of the settlement was the deep blue sea and to the north and west, the Banks, a vast expanse of shallow green water. North, behind Mond's settlement, was a mysterious pine forest. It was a place of superstition and fear, where only the bravest went. The farm that Mond and Uncle Willie tended was at the edge of the forest, behind the settlement. One hot summer day, Mond and Uncle Willie ran out of water for the plants. So, Mond took a bucket and set out to find some.

Without realizing it, he wandered into the forest, and was soon lost. Mond was determined to find water and return to the farm, but he couldn't find the way back. He wandered about for hours until he found himself on the rocky rim of a deep-water ocean hole. There was a rock in the middle and a naked lady was sitting on it combing her hair. She wasn't aware of Mond until he gasped out loud and dropped the bucket. She slowly put down her comb and looked directly at Mond. Then, with one deft movement, she slid off the rock into the water.

Mond waited a long time for the lady to resurface, but she never did. As he sat waiting, he noticed something glinting in the sunlight on the rock. He dove into the pond, swam swiftly to the rock, and climbed out shivering with fright.

A strange looking seashell lay on the rock, and with a trembling hand Mond picked it up.
He somehow found his way back to the farm and showed the shell to his uncle. When Uncle Willie examined it and listened to Mond's story, he exclaimed, "Mond, that lady was a mermaid, and this is her comb! You are a lucky boy! There are two things that live in ocean holes," Uncle Willie explained, "Dupees and Mermaids."

Mond looked puzzled. So, his uncle continued, "Dupees are evil monsters and they will eat you if they get the chance, but mermaids are different. They help people." Uncle Willie paused and smiled. "I believe in those things, but in my whole life, I've never seen a mermaid." That was saying a lot, because Uncle Willie was eighty years old and he had sailed around the world on a whaling ship!

Mond and Uncle Willie went back to the ocean hole and waited all night, hoping to see the mermaid. Mond had the comb and he was ready to throw it to her if she returned, but she never did. Mond wanted to give her the comb. He knew he shouldn't have taken it.

"Keep the comb," Uncle Willie advised. "She might have left it for you to take. Mermaids do strange things sometimes. They are magical creatures, and the comb may have magic too."

At dawn they walked home. Mond showed the comb to his family and everyone in the settlement.

For years afterwards, people came from all over the island to see the wondrous Mermaid's Comb.

When Mond was fifteen, Uncle Willie gave up farming and bought a sailboat. They began a new life on the sea. They set fish traps, hooked sponges, netted turtles, and harvested lobsters and conchs. It was a good life for Mond, and he learned quickly. Soon, he could handle the sailboat as well as his uncle. He could tell the depth of water and predict weather by observing the sea and sky.

As a young man, Uncle Willie had been a smack-boat fisherman, and he taught Mond everything he knew about the sea. At night, they would sit on deck under the stars. Uncle Willie would feed Mond's imagination with tales of sea monsters, ocean storms, and shipwrecks. His stories were not always true, but Mond could tell which were and weren't by the twinkle in his uncle's eyes. Uncle Willie told Mond about cities of steel and glass, where people drove shiny cars, about snow at Christmas, and about children who had never seen the ocean. "Or a mermaid either," Mond, who had never seen a city or snow would say with pride.

"Few souls have seen what you have," Uncle Willie said. "You were blessed by that mermaid." Ever since he took the comb, Mond had kept it close at hand, in case he saw the mermaid again. At times, he would walk inland to the ocean hole, but the rock would always be empty. "Someday," Uncle Willie predicted, "She will need that comb, and she'll come for it."

One fine Autumn day, Mond and Uncle Willie set sail for the fishing grounds with a porpoise rolling in the boat's wake. That afternoon, a violent storm came up. It blew full gale day and night, and by morning they were far out on the banks. The wind had died away. There was only the blue sky above and the green shallows all around them. No land was in sight. Mond climbed the mast for a better look, but saw nothing. Uncle Willie looked at the clear sky and empty horizon and shook his head. "We're lost," he said with a laugh. "Just like you were when you found the ocean hole."

"What'll we do?" Mond asked. "There's no wind. So, we can't sail."

"Nothing," Uncle Willie answered. "We'll have to stay anchored and wait for the wind."

They waited at anchor for four flat calm days and their water gave out. They fished with no luck and there was no sign of wind.

"We're lost for sure," Uncle Willie declared. "God save us!"

Then, early one morning, Mond heard something scraping the bottom of the boat. He hurried on deck and looked over the side. To his surprise a dolphin was there looking up at him.

"Hello," the dolphin said. "I know you are lost. So, I have come to lead you home."

Mond thought he was dreaming. "How do you know we're lost?" he asked.

The dolphin smiled, rolled over, and looked at Mond with one eye. "I have followed you for many days. So, I know," he replied with a wink.

By then, Uncle Willie was on deck listening. He wasn't at all surprised that Mond and the dolphin were carrying on a conversation. He believed in such things.

"When you lived on land," the dolphin said, "You were kind to the birds and you fed the lizards. The Mermaid saw all of that." The dolphin continued, "When you went to sea, she had me follow you and keep you safe." He smiled as all dolphins do. "And it seems you're in trouble now," he said. Mond was too full of wonder to speak.

"Come now," the dolphin said, "Raise your anchor. There's a fair wind. So, set sail and follow me!"

They followed the dolphin to the island and Mond gave him the comb. Uncle Willie asked the dolphin why the mermaid didn't come for it herself. There was no reply, only a swirl of water, and the dolphin was gone. Mond shook his head as if to clear it of a dream. He turned to his uncle. "I know why she didn't come," he said. "I was lucky to have seen her once in my life, and that's the way she wanted it."

BAHAMA SPONGE SCHOONER OF THE 1930's
NO.   OF 50 BY WM JOHNSON, JR.

BUTTERFLY DREAMS

If you dream you're a butterfly, then perhaps, there's a butterfly dreaming it's you.

YUCATAN

The Mexican state of Quintana Roo has a number of Mayan pyramids, Tulum and Chichinitza being well known and popular with tourists. One of the largest pyramids is Uxmal in the jungle interior.

My girlfriend and I visited Uxmal when it was being studied by anthropologists and excavated by archaeologists. I bribed a security guard to let us into the pyramid, and at sunset we climbed the steep narrow stone steps to the altar at the top. There, we spread out our sleeping bags.

It was a moonless, windy night with low scudding clouds. A cold front was on the way. We spent the night on the floor beside the altar, and needless to say we didn't sleep very well.

We knew about the thousands of sacrifices that had taken place on the altar. Hearts had been cut from living bodies. Sacrificial blood had flowed over the altar and down the stone steps.

Spirits of the dead disturbed our dreams that night, until the light of day dispersed them. We stood on the top of Uxmal Pyramid, watching the sunrise over the green jungle canopy. Then we made love to reaffirm life.

After Uxmal, we spent three days in Merida, waiting for the train from Mexico City. We got to know our taxi driver Nesiem, a member of the Palastine Arab community in Merida. It was a large, politically active community of Palestinian Arabs. They even had a daily newspaper in Arabic.

On our last night in Merida, Nesiem invited us to dinner with his family. The next day, he delivered us to the train. The 'Rapido' as it was called had a Pullman car, where we were given a luxurious compartment. There was no dining car and no porters on the Rapido. Passengers had to supply their own food for the two-day trip to Mexico City.

The first morning, the train ran on trestles over swamp land, and in the afternoon, across grassy savannas, and then into foothills.

That night, we shared our food with a destitute family on their way to the city to find work.

The next day we were in the high mountains. By afternoon, we had circled Orizaba volcano and were coming down into the valley of Mexico.

NOTE: There is now a hotel at Uxmal to accommodate visitors.

Pl. V
© 1999. W.R.J., Jr.

118

CONCH LIME
The Burn Pile

In the days when inter-island freight service was infrequent, and at times non-existent, there was a need for cement and plaster. Bahamians solved this problem by using conch lime. It was made in a unique way. A post of buttonwood was driven into the ground and a rope was tied to it as a radius by which a circle of 30 or 40 feet was scribed on the ground. Within the circle, dry brush and wood was laid down, and then a layer of conch shells. Another layer of kindling was laid over the conch shells, and so on, in alternating layers of wood and shells, until the circular pile was eight or ten feet high.

Building a burn pile took much labour and a profusion of conch shells. On completion, it was covered with palm thatch to keep it dry. When there was a calm day, usually in winter, after the passing of a cold front, the pile would be set afire. It would burn and smoulder for weeks as the calcium of the shells became calcium carbonate (lime).

When the pile burned down and cooled, the ashes would be raked. The ashes were gathered and used as mortar. On the walls of many Out Island houses one can still see streaks of grey and pink from the conch lime. It is thought that the traditional Bahamian pink colour derives from this.

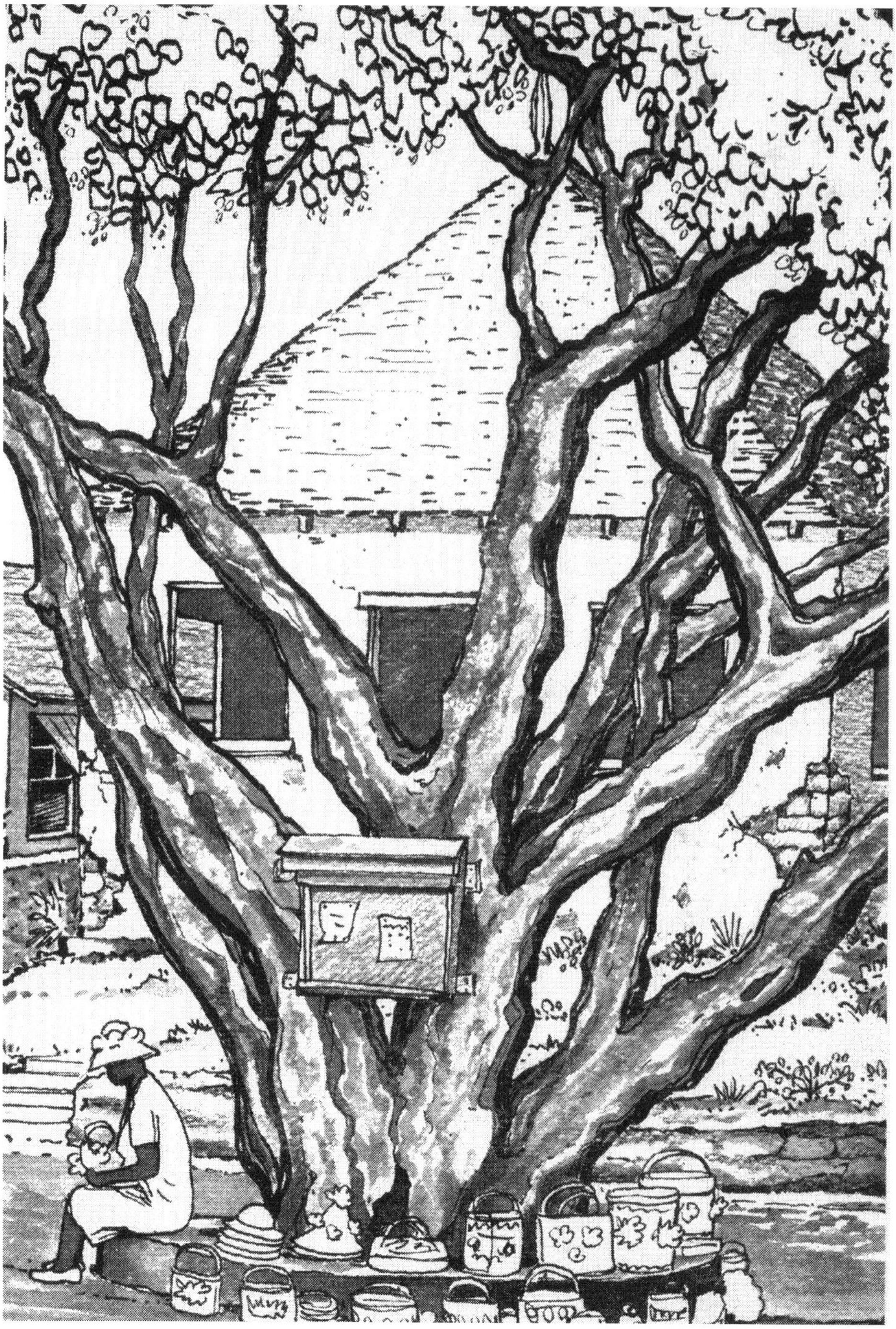

GORDON SMITH

During a trip to Toronto, I had an encounter that made a lasting impression on me. It was a snow-bound February day in the suburbs of the city. My girlfriend and I were having coffee in a deserted diner.

An old man was sitting alone by the front window, staring out at the snow-covered street. My girlfriend felt sorry for the man sitting all alone, and she invited him to join us.

What ensued was this:

He said he was an artist on his way to visit his dying wife in the hospital. He told us of his youth in Canada, of marrying his childhood sweetheart, and how they saved every penny for a trip to the South Seas. He had been enthusiastic and idealistic in his youth with hopes of becoming a great artist. He dreamed of capturing the same beauty that Paul Gauguin immortalized in oils.

The young couple took a train to Vancouver and boarded a tramp steamer for Tahiti. He bought his wife a second-class ticket because they couldn't afford first class, and he made the trip in steerage.

On reaching Tahiti, they took a trading schooner to the island of Rarotonga where he began painting.

One day while walking on the reef, he was cut by the coral and his leg infected. They were forced to return home to Canada. His dream of painting Paradise was never realized.

When the man finished his story he stood, thanked us for the coffee and wished us well. As he walked away, my girlfriend ran to him and gave him a warm hug. When he got to the door, the man turned, and with tears in his eyes he waved goodbye.

VERSE:
He went in steerage to the Gauguin Isles,
so his first-class lady could go second class.
From a tropic clime they sailed to Paradise
where under the tropic sun he brushed wet images on thirsty paper

Chance encounters came and went, and he met my heroes there when I was only five (Robert Dean Frisbie, James Norman Hall, and Robert Gibbings)
He returned home when I was six, beaten by the reef.
Years later on a snow-bound day, our fan-shaped paths converged in friendly words and coffee.
    His failing eyes fed my soul with gifts of remembrance, and a girl's embrace pleasured him with needed warmth

Note: After leaving Polynesia, Frisbie's daughter ended her life singing in Japanese nightclubs under her given name of Whiskey Johnnie.

BAHAMA BARE-HEAD SMACK
BY Wm JOHNSON, JR. © 1974 & © 2000

SHERLOCK HACKLEY

It was 1958 and there had been an attempted assassination of Francois Duvalier, the president of Haiti. Duvalier had declared a State of Siege. Property was being seized and his opponents were being arrested and executed. Chaos reigned in Haiti!

My father's friend, Sherlock Hackley owned and operated a two-plane charter air service, and when Poppa Doc threatened to nationalize all foreign-owned property, Sherlock flew his aircraft out of the country.

He offered to fly me out as well, but I declined, because my boat, Island Girl, was anchored at Port de Paix. The next day, I sailed her north to the safety of Inagua Island in the Bahamas.

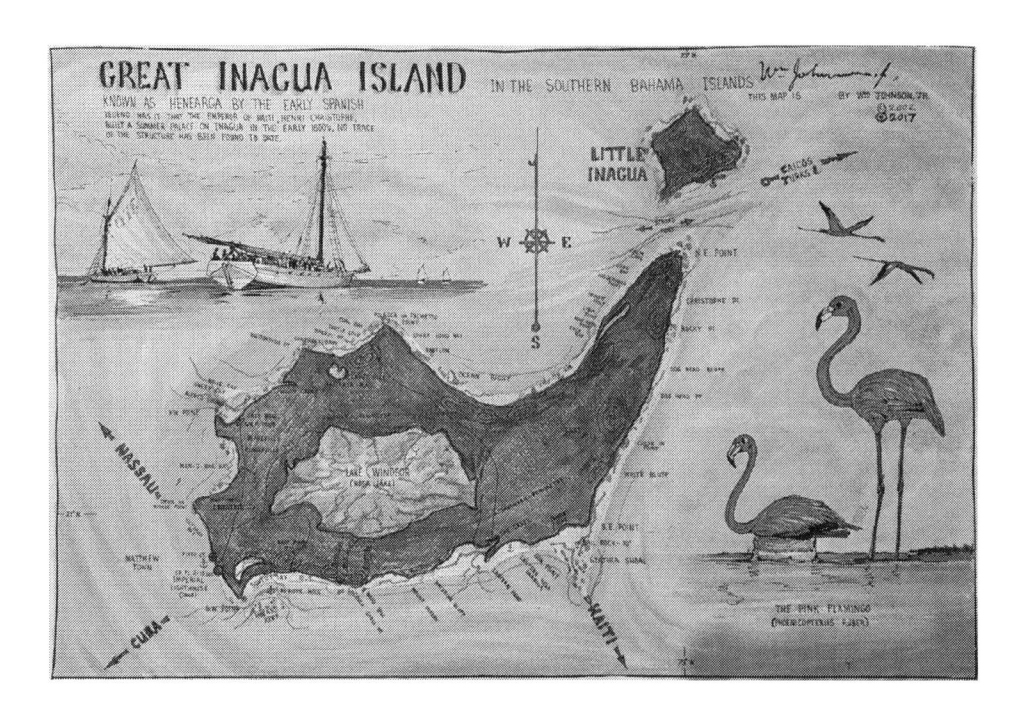

ON RETIRING FROM THE SEA

Boats are now made of fiberglass, not wood; the art of navigation has been replaced by electronics, and there are no more sailors, only yachtsmen. For me, the romance and challenge of the sea is gone. I have to accept the fact that all things change, and that nothing lasts forever…

We survived hurricane Andrew in 1992 and moved the houseboat back to the rebuilt marina, but I became restless. I wanted more! I wanted time to live and enjoy life.

I was living in Miami with Ripple the cat, writing and doing artwork. I was living well but achieving nothing of significance.

As a child, I always felt there was a beach for me somewhere in the islands, so at the age of 66, I made an important life decision. I would build a home in the islands I love and live there the rest of my life being productive.

A week before Christmas, I flew to Abaco and found a parcel of land overlooking the sea and backed by cliffs and caves. I purchased it and returned to Miami where I set to work getting together everything I would need to build and furnish my future home. I drew plans and built a scale model of the proposed house. I wanted it to be a place that could withstand hurricanes, a home that would be cozy in winter and a windswept refuge in summer. I planned the house I had always dreamed of, a sailor's refuge.

Note: In olden days when a sailor retired from the sea, he would put an oar on his shoulder and walk inland until someone asked, "What's that on your shoulder?" There he would make his home.

Back in Miami, I bought a gas refrigerator, a stove, a small generator, a table saw, chop saw, router, half-inch drill, a circular saw, and all the tools and equipment I would need. I filled the Tortuga houseboat with all the gear I would need in Abaco. My most important purchase was a series of solar panels, a regulator, and an inverter to power my future home. In the meantime, they powered Tortuga. When all was in order, I arranged with a friend to tow Tortuga to Abaco with his Biscayne Bay tugboat. We made a rope bridle to prevent yawing under tow, and at midnight May 20th 1997, we departed Miami for Abaco.

It was a calm moonlit night in the Gulf Stream with long low swells and a gentle southwest wind to give us a boost. Ripple and I were aboard Tortuga while my friend towed us with his tug boat. Towing an engineless houseboat across the Gulf Stream was a gamble, but it paid off.

After an uneventful nine-hour run along the axis of the Gulf Stream, we reached Grand Bahama at dawn and motored in past Indian Cay. We crossed the Little Bahama Banks to Great Sale Cay, where we spent the second night. Poor Ripple was seasick the whole way across, throwing up, eating, and then throwing up again. He hated the noise of the tugboat's engine, and he was profoundly unhappy with the turn his life was taking.

A few years before, Ripple and I had gone through hurricane Andrew and he was still traumatized, so that any change in his life affected him physically.

We must have looked like some sort of gypsy refugee boat with all our gear tied on the upper deck, a bicycle lashed to the rails, and the 17-foot Mud Hen athwart the afterdeck.

From Great Sale Cay we went on to Manjack Cay where we launched the Mud Hen and sailed around for a while. Next morning, the wind piped up from the northeast. We weighed anchor and ran on to the Customs Wharf in Marsh Harbour. As planned, we arrived there at three pm on a Friday afternoon, just when they were closing for the weekend. Within an hour, the authorities had accepted my inventory of goods to be imported, I had paid the duty, and we were cleared. Customs never even asked for Ripple's health certificate that I had gone to so much trouble to obtain.

That afternoon, Tortuga was towed across the Sea of Abaco to Sea Spray Marina where I met Monty and Ruth Albury, the owners.

Ripple and I were to live there for the next two years while I built our home.

As soon as Tortuga was tied to the sea wall by Sea Spray, Ripple took off exploring. I worried that he might jump ship permanently after such a traumatic journey, but that night he returned. The next day, Monty gave us a slip in the Marina.

Ripple seemed as well as ever after three days of seasickness, and from then on, he established his territory at Sea Spray. He fought with the tough Elbow Cay cats and occasionally fell overboard in the process, but he always managed to climb the pilings and return to the boat.

During the building of Casa Tortuga, I slept on the hard floor in the main cabin with Ripple beside me. He ran in and out all night to roam the marina and fight. Many a night, I awoke with a wet cat sitting on my back washing itself. I didn't worry about Ripple falling overboard until one full-moon night, as I was urinating over the side, a bull shark emerged from the shadow of the boat.

After Monty built the Garbanzo Bar, two feral cats took up residence under the deck, and Ripple began spending time there doing Tomcat things. Many epic fights occurred there, much to the amusement of the Sea Spray guests and staff. Day and night, screeches and yowls could be heard from under the deck, but soon Ripple was victorious. He was known to many of the boaters as a fighter and a loner, a cat who never begged food from anyone. Ripple knew where food and home were, and he always returned to the sanctuary of the houseboat.

Ripple was so feared by the Garbanzo cats that they brought in some muscle in the form of a tough and ragged Tomcat, an experienced street fighter. Ripple defeated him in an epic skirmish and he never came back.

Ripple had a reputation for attacking any dog that came down the dock. One day he backed a Rottweiler into the water, and another time he chased Big Max, the Labrador, around the bar and down the road. Everyone had a good laugh at that, but I felt sorry for old Max. He was a gentle dog and he only wanted to be friendly.

Ripple saw me off every day before dawn as I sailed away in the Mud Hen to the building site on Lubbers Quarters. In the evening, Ripple greeted me when I returned. He would be on the foredeck to give me the love treatment by rubbing the railing and kissing me as I came aboard.

Those years at Sea Spray with Ripple were some of my happiest. There was satisfying hard physical labour each day, a bath at Tahiti Beach on the way home, then aboard the houseboat, exhausted and hungry with my companion Ripple.

When the weather was too bad to sail to Lubbers, I would hang out at the bar and play dominoes with Mizpah, the bartender and Norris, the chef. Ripple would be under the deck, within the sound of my voice. Spike, the marina dog, would be at the bar begging food from the guests.

Spike and Ripple maintained an easy truce by staying at least 6 feet apart at all times. Ripple hated all dogs, but he tolerated Spike because I fed her and kept peace between them. Any other dog in the area was fresh meat for my Tomcat.

One day, Ripple met a rooster in the bush, and the encounter turned into a comical Mexican standoff. The rooster clucked menacingly and kicked up dirt while Ripple gnashed his teeth and howled. There was no retreat for either of them until I broke it up.

Now, years later, with Ripple gone, Spike recognizes me when I visit Sea Spray, and I'm reminded of all those good times there on the dock.

I was younger then, strong and proud of my Spartan lifestyle. Those were Halcyon days of sun, sand, and sea, walking windswept beaches on distant islands, running bare-foot on the rocks, and tasting life to the fullest.

When I first saw that piece of land at Lubbers, I resolved to build there. It was obvious from the start that it would be difficult to build on property that rose from a low rocky shore to a heavily wooded area, some 40 feet above sea level. Two giant rocks were on mid-property, and I knew from the start that it would be difficult to situate the house among them. "Dynamite those rocks," I was told by the locals in Hope Town. "Otherwise you won't be able to build there." But from the start, I was determined to save those parts of the cliffs that fell there thousands of years ago. Little did I know then, that my property had an ancient history dating back to the ice ages and to pre-Columbian times.

In the caves and all around in the soil, there are white conch shells, each with a small hole where Bahamians make slits to remove the animal. In the caves, there are thousands of those shells overlain by more recent ones with the characteristic Bahamian slit.

For over two years, I worked building Casa Tortuga. It was hard work carrying all the supplies, tools, cement, and lumber from the shore, up the steep hill to the building site. The only sections of the house that I did not build myself were the foundations (half of which encloses an 8000-gallon rainwater cistern), and the six-inch-thick, 20 by 30-foot concrete floor slab. Freddy Jones, Jr. and his crew did all that for me. After I staked out the house, I hired three gravediggers from Bain Town to cut trenches in the bedrock. They used axes and hand-held pole drills.

When the trenches were done, we drove rebars into the bedrock and poured in cement. The foundations were well-locked onto bedrock. We were ready to block up the cistern walls. The floor slab would be on top of the cistern and the house on top of that.

Freddy and his crew arrived on site and we spent a month mixing concrete for the foundations, blocking up cistern walls, and pouring structural columns. In those days, there was no concrete mixer or electricity on Lubbers Quarters. So, all mixing was done by hand. It was extremely hot that summer, but I had a hard-working crew and all went well.

When I was pouring the belt course, I cut my hand on a rebar and bled into the wet cement. Now Casa Tortuga is a physical part of me.

FLOYD

That fall hurricane Floyd ran the length of Abaco, destroying homes, sinking boats and eroding land. The profiles of many islands were changed forever. Tahiti Beach was altered drastically. Luckily, no lives were lost.

In White Sound, the Sea Spray docks were uprooted and twisted. The ridge east of Sound was eroded down to sea level, exposing the Atlantic Ocean to view.

Casa Tortuga came through with only minor damage and the loss of one solar panel.

At the height of the storm, my neighbour's roof collapsed. He and his dog and David, his servant, cut their way through the bush and climbed in the bathroom window. They were our guests for the next ten weeks. Ripple was not at all happy with a dog in his house.

Any boat that had not been hauled out was sunk. Maggie ended up on top of the destroyed Mud Hen. Luckily, I had sold the houseboat to Rocky and Darvis the week before Floyd. It was weeks before all the debris was cleared, reconstruction was under way, and things were back to normal.

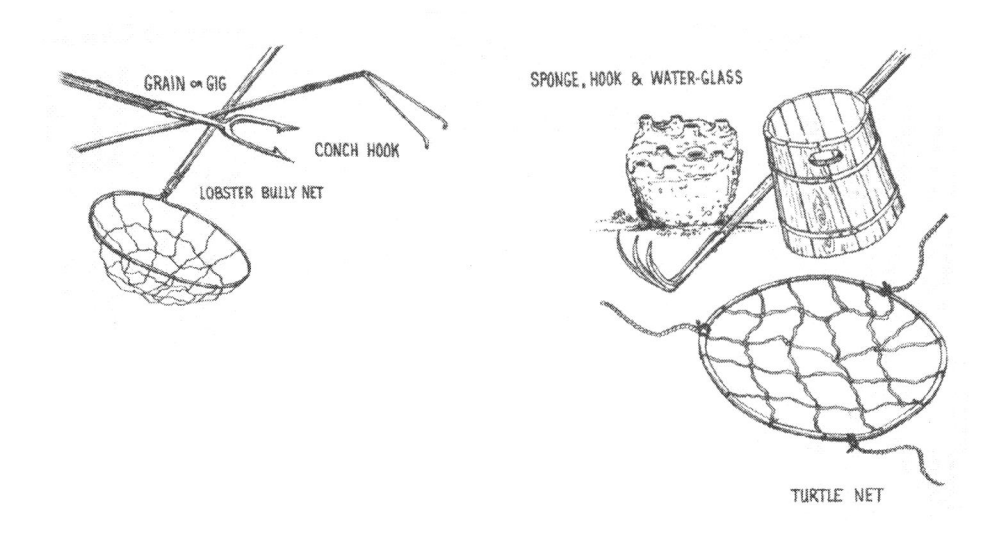

FLOOR SLAB

I determined we would need a concrete mixer, so I ordered a self-powered one from Canada. When it arrived in Marsh Harbour and was cleared by customs, the Abacays barge delivered it to Lubbers, and I set about assembling the cement, sand, gravel and re-bars.

As it turned out, the mixer wasn't enough for all the concrete we would need. So, when the forms and re-bars were laid and wired, and it came time to pour the floor slab, we had to hand-mix on plywood sheets alongside the mixer. Freddy got together seventeen workers, and we commenced at dawn the week before Christmas.

It took fourteen hours to pour the floor slab. We mixed the concrete on the shore, and formed a bucket brigade from there to the base of a fifteen-foot ladder at the southeast corner of the cistern. Each bucket was passed up the ladder and walked diagonally across the re-barred floor to the northwest corner where the pouring began. Because of the steepness of the site, the northwest corner was nearly at grade level, whereas the southeast ladder corner was fifteen feet high. When we finished pouring and smoothing the slab, it was dark. So, the final work was lit by kerosene lanterns. That night everyone went home exhausted.

It was dark when I sailed back to Sea Spray. Ripple met me as usual when I tied up to the foredeck. I was exhausted and I spent a restless night dreaming of returning the next day to find the floor slab collapsed into the cistern.

Ripple saw me off before dawn, and when I reached the site, I walked across the hard concrete slab to the northwest corner where there were footprints of a wild cat in the cement. They are there today beneath my couch-bed where I have the large battery that powers the house.

An amusing incident occurred during the cutting of the foundation trench. I was away for the morning in Marsh Harbour, and when I sailed into the bay in front of the site, I heard shouts and screams from my gravedigger crew. I ran up the hill to find the men running around in a panic. They had seen a bees' nest in the cliffs above, so they built a crude ladder, lit a torch and climbed up to it.

Resenting the intrusion, the bees attacked, the ladder broke, and the men panicked. Luckily no one was hurt, only a few bee stings but no honey.)

When the floor slab was finished, Freddy's crew left and I was alone with my project. I began stockpiling concrete blocks, re-bar, sand, and cement, but first I built the porch and stairs and attached three ten-by-ten wooden posts to the east wall of the cistern.

When Abacays delivered to the harbour, I carried the cement blocks and lumber across the beach and up the hill to the floor slab. In those days there were no trucks on the island.

For two years I mixed mortar, poured concrete columns, and laid up block walls. There were scratches and bruises and I broke two fingers. The north wall is my winter wall. The book shelf wall has no window. The west wall has a large double window and a single large window, as well as a tall bathroom window. At the east corner of the south wall is a kitchen window.

After I hand-mixed and poured the concrete columns and belt course, I framed out the roof, covered it with lapped half-inch plywood, and sealed it with several coats of elastomeric roof paint. All the bolts and lines were hot-dipped galvanized iron. I used stainless steel ring nails only. The hurricane rafter ties were of galvanized iron, and they began to rust after hurricane Floyd. They have since been replaced by heavy-duty stainless-steel ties.

The shed roof slopes upward to the west to a four-foot-high wooden wall above the belt course. I wanted a cool house with an air flow even on light wind days. So, there are three vent windows in the middle of the upper back wall. They draw radiant heat from under the roof, and the sea air in from the screened porch. The hot air is drawn in by convection, so that on hot days, even when there's no sea breeze, there is a flow of air. This is a magical place. Lucayan spirits inhabit the land. Their voices are waves on an iron shore.

My house is oriented north-south, and I sleep with my head to the north. I watch the sun and moon rise over Cooperjack Cay, and at night I see Polaris above the cliffs.

The year we moved into the finished house Hurricane Floyd struck Abaco, destroying homes, sinking boats, and eroding land.

Ripple and I came through without a scratch, but a year later, Ripple died of feline leukemia. He is buried under the cliffs, where bluebells and yellow elder flowers fall. Now, with the house finished, I sleep alone in silent windswept wonder, thinking of Ripple.

DORIAN

BEFORE THE STORM
There were pixies in the palm trees and mermaids in the sea.
It was a time for joy and laughter, a time for you and me.

THE STORM
A raging wind denied us joy and storm surge killed the laughter.
The world changed then for ever after.

AFTER THE STORM
Now's a time for mending, to build and regain our loss.
A new and better time for all of us.

AL'S MISTAKE

I must tell the story of my friend Al Bruno, an accomplished ship's carpenter and a profoundly innocent soul.

Al lived aboard a gaff-rigged cutter in Havana Harbour, and each morning he went to a nearby diner for empanadas and breakfast. That's where he practiced his Spanish. Al was bound and determined to learn the language. So, the night before, he would go through a dictionary and put together the necessary words to order breakfast and make small talk with the diner's patrons and staff.

One fateful morning, Al walked into the diner, sat down at the counter, and said to the waitress, "Tengo dos huevos." The waitress blushed and the restaurant erupted in laughter. Al was trying to say, "I want two eggs." Instead he said, "I *have* two eggs."

He should have said, "Quiero dos huevos." Instead, he said I have two cojones, a slang form of macho bragging.

After the mistake was explained, Al never again attempted to speak Spanish.

Many people, when learning a foreign language, are self-conscious about making embarrassing mistakes. Al was certainly one of them after that incident in Old Havana.

ANN-LOUISE THE LEBANESE
A Mystery Solved

Some years ago in college, I became romantically involved with a young architecture student named Ann-Louise. She was known on campus as "Ann-Louise, the Lebanese." She was a strikingly voluptuous, dark-haired beauty, and the desire of every man.

For some reason she was attracted to me, and we commenced a torrid, year-long affair that evolved from petting to the inevitable attempt at intercourse.

The only problem (and this was the mystery) was that her vagina could not be penetrated. I could barely insert my little finger.

Naturally, it was frustrating for both of us, but nothing could be done about it. We indulged in everything short of penetration and our frustration grew.

Ann-Louise admitted she was a virgin, and I understood why. Our affair finally ended in friendship and mutual frustration, and I never saw her again.

Recently, while reading a paper on female circumcision, I came across descriptions of suture and infibulation, and the mystery was solved. I never knew what religion Ann-Louise embraced, but she was definitely of Arab descent and probably a Muslim. I believe now that she was sutured as a child to ensure her virginity.

ATLANTIC AVENUE
Brooklyn

One Indian-summer day, there was a street fair on Atlantic Avenue. There were tables and racks of goods for sale; some of it new but most of it old. At the time, every sensory input had significance for me. On one of the tables there were piles of dog-eared books and among them a photo album. It was full of faded photographs of "old country" people, perhaps Italians or Greeks. They were snap-shots and studio photographs of self-conscious stiffly posed men and women. Dour gentlemen in starched collars, sporting handlebar moustaches stood with their women beside them. There were pictures of children and babies, and studio photos of families posed in ordered array. There were widows and spinsters in mourning lace with sad eyes that told of pain and loss.

For a moment, I considered purchasing that unwanted chronicle of someone's life; of all its joys, hopes and hurts, but I could not. It was too emotionally overwhelming. So, I replaced the tattered album on the table, thanked God for my own life, and walked away into the crowd on Atlantic Avenue.

That day I found a greater appreciation of life and love.

ISLAND ARCHITECTURE

In past times, houses in the out islands were built of native rock. Conch lime was used for mortar. Forms were erected and rock and mortar were poured in to make a rubble wall. When the forms were removed, conch lime plaster was applied. After that, a thatched or shingled roof was built.

If milled lumber was available, wooden houses were often built. Doors, window frames, and shutters were made of wood. Most family homes had only one or two rooms. Screen wire was generally unavailable or too expensive. So, doors and windows were closed at night and cedar chips and coconut oil were burned as a bug repellent. The floors of the houses were either tamped earth or wooden planking.

In the capital of Nassau, where there was relative prosperity and materials at hand, large wooden houses were constructed. Rock was sawn from local limestone quarries for the walls and foundations.

On islands where boatbuilding was carried out, there arose a tradition of wooden house construction. There are examples of those houses at Governor's Harbour and Harbour Island, Eleuthera, and in the Abacos. In those houses, it's obvious the joinery work was done by shipwrights, and in some cases natural crook knees were used for bracing. Those houses have stood for many years and weathered severe hurricanes, a testament to the skill of their builders.

Descendants of the Loyalist settlers here in the islands have carried on the tradition of high-pitched roofs. Several examples of these may be seen today in Eleuthera and Abaco.

One of the most unique and innovative designs that adapts the high-pitched roof to our semi-tropical environment is at Tarpum Bay, Eleuthera. I have seen this design only at Tarpum Bay, with one exception. A house at South Palmetto Point was built by a man for his wife who was born at Tarpum Bay. She wanted a home like the one she was raised in. So, he built it for her as a testament of his love!

This unique design allows for both ventilation and the utilization of attic space for living quarters. Each gable end of a large high-pitched roof is left open, with a recessed wall six or eight feet in. A porch is thus formed at either end of the attic. Railings are added to the porches, and doorways and windows are cut in the recessed walls. On larger structures, dormer windows are added to the roof.

THE LUCERNE HOTEL

The Lucerne Hotel was built during the sponging boom of the nineteen hundreds. By the 1990s, its paint was peeling and it was riddled with termites and dry rot. Time had not been kind to the old structure.

Shipwrights planked the hotel with first-growth Abaco pine and used horseflesh and madeira hardwoods for braces and structural knees.

In a high wind, the building creaks and groans like a restless old man. Captain Sawyer, the owner, insists it was built that way on purpose. "She adapts to the wind stress, and she works like a ship's hull in a seaway," he says.

The Captain is proud of his decaying relic, and he refers to it as 'She', like sailors do their ships. Like a traditional sailing vessel, the Lucerne is well proportioned and a classic of Bahamian design. The design of the hotel has its rooms around a three-story central atrium open to the sky, and that sunlit core is a veritable sounding box. One can stand on the inside balcony of any floor and hear people talking two floors away.

BARON ERNEST RITTER Von KREIDNER

He was a cabin boy in the Kaiser's navy during the First World War and later on, an admiral in the Chilean navy. When I knew him, he had a classic car dealership in Palm Beach and was active in sports car racing. He competed with Briggs Cunningham (2 litre 1935 Ferrari), Freddy Whacker, and the brothers Sam and Miles Collier, sons of Barron Collier.

Ernie's flamboyance was legendary. He competed in a Jaguar XK, wearing a leather aviator's helmet, goggles, and a flowing white scarf. Win or lose, at the finish of every race, there was a bottle of champagne. He had two teenage Puerto Rican boys as pit crew, and he referred to them as his "wards." The fact surfaced later, that Von Kreidner was a dedicated paedophile.

BLIND CHESS
From Esperansa

There was a time in Neil Gardiner's life, after Pati's death and his return to Nassau, when he could not bear to face the end of day. It depressed him because he thought of sunset as an end of life, like death. Dawn, however, he considered a rebirth, the beginning of life. It took Johnnie Boeuf a month and a number of chess games to cure Neil of his phobia.

When Neil first told his friend of his fear of sunsets, John laughed and said he had a theory about people who live where they see the sunrise. They are invariably optimistic, whereas those who see it set every day tend to be pessimistic.

"What about those who live on small islands or on the sea?" Neil asked. "Those exposed to sunrise *and* sunset?"

"I suppose they are the schizophrenics!" John answered grinning and he added, "It's interesting how my theory fits in with your phobia. You've always been a positive thinking guy because you're a sunrise person and now you abhor the end of day."

"At least I'm not a 'schizo?'" Neil joked.

John shook his head, laughed and went on talking. He was on one of his philosophic rants that Neil knew so well. "My theory holds up when you realize that a person living on the Atlantic coast of North America is usually more conservative and positive thinking than his counterpart on the Pacific coast." John waited for a comment from Neil, but there was only a smile. "Consider the politics and attitude differences between Floridians and Californians. They are polar opposites!"

On the spur of the moment, John could come up with theories on any subject. They were always interesting, sometimes humorous, but not necessarily logical. John's sunrise/sunset theory amused Neil, but he was too kind to laugh or criticise.

John was a chess master who learned the game in China during the nineteen-thirties. Neil was an accomplished chess player, but he was no match for John. They often played on the porch at Don's East Bay house. It was a dawn porch, open to the north and east with a view of the sea and Nassau Harbour that was obscured by walls on the south and west. Don's porch knew only morning.

Late one afternoon, Neil and John were on Don's dock, watching the smack boats sailing in from a day on the Yellow Banks. The sun was low and Neil was getting restless. He headed for the house.

"Hold on!" John said, "Let's play a chess game before you go.

"How can we?" Neil retorted, pointing at the house. "The board's up there on the porch."

John smiled. "Let me explain," he said, and he told Neil how they could play chess by calling the moves to each other while visualizing the board. Before Neil could object, John called an opening move. Neil thought for a moment and called a move. John called another, and after a thoughtful pause, Neil advanced his queen's pawn. The mind-game was underway! Two hours later when the game ended in a decisive checkmate by John, the sun had set and it was getting dark. Neil had been so absorbed in their game that he had not noticed the end of day.

Every evening after that, the two friends sat on Don's dock smoking pot, drinking rum, and playing blind chess. Soon, Neil could easily visualize the chess pieces on his mental board, and once, he check-mated John.

Neil's greatest triumph, however, was his newfound ability to ignore the setting sun.

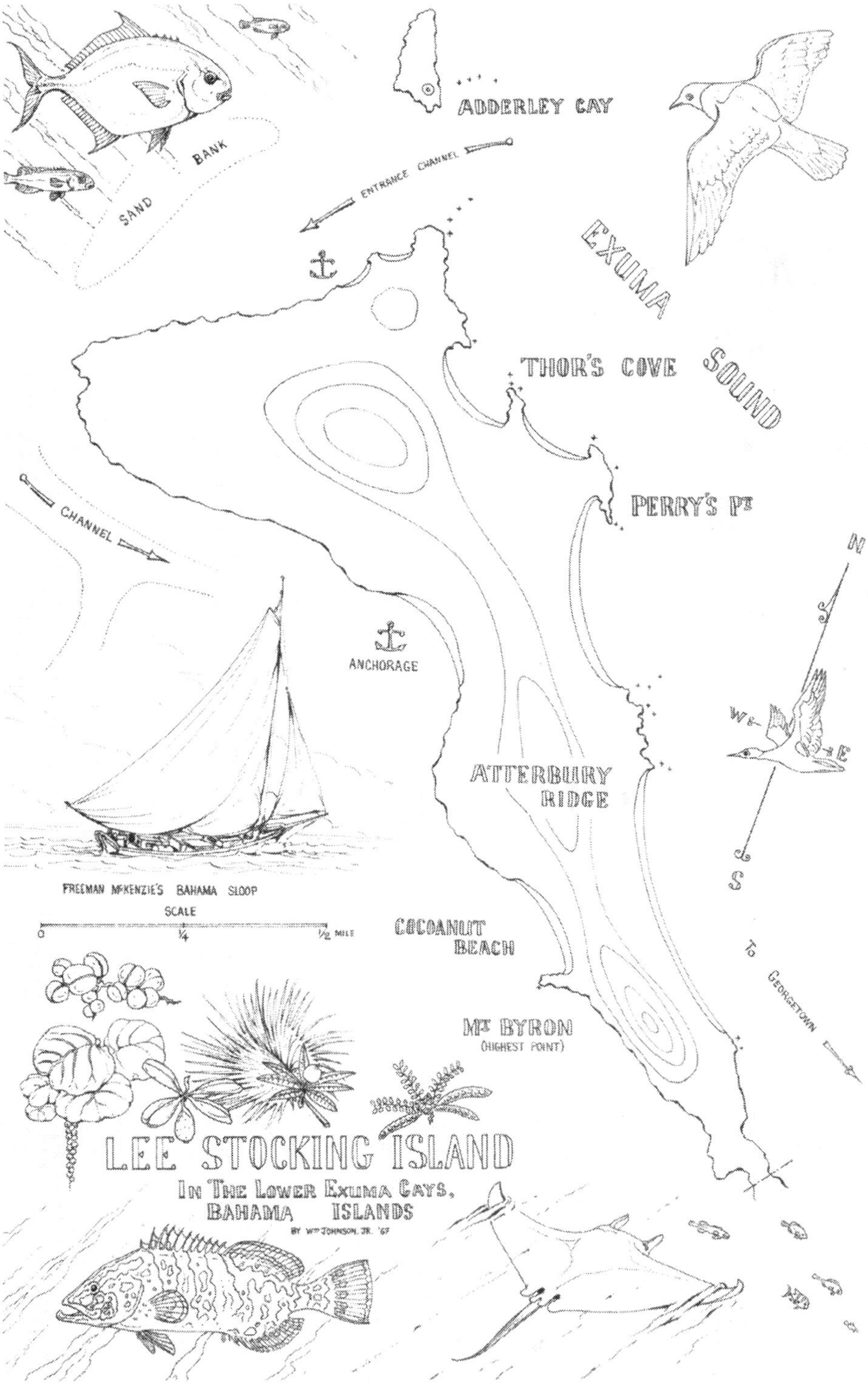
ADDERLEY CAY
ENTRANCE CHANNEL
SAND BANK
EXUMA SOUND
THOR'S COVE
PERRY'S Pt
CHANNEL
ANCHORAGE
ATTERBURY RIDGE
N
S
W
E
FREEMAN McKENZIE'S BAHAMA SLOOP
SCALE
0 1/4 1/2 MILE
COCOANUT BEACH
TO GEORGETOWN
Mt BYRON
(HIGHEST POINT)
LEE STOCKING ISLAND
IN THE LOWER EXUMA CAYS, BAHAMA ISLANDS
BY Wm JOHNSON, JR. '67

FREDDIE'S WAY

Freddie Whey was an obsessive individual who devoted total energy and enthusiasm to whatever he was into. During the Hippie era, Freddy's creative energies were devoted entirely to the music of the day.

I first met Freddy in Coconut Grove, during his abstract painting period. His works were being exhibited and they were selling quite well. That was before he painted himself out and retired from the art world.

The Grove in those days was an obscure little village on the outskirts of Miami, not the trendy artsy-crafty place it is today. Freddie was going through a red period in his abstract paintings. At first, they were in every shade of red, from dark crimson to blood red. Then they got lighter in colour until they were a barely discernible pink. That was prior to his blue period and the yellow period that began with dark yellow and evolved into such a brilliant yellow that it hurt the eyes. Freddy worked his way through the entire colour spectrum producing a prodigious number of canvases.

I was walking past Freddie's house one day when he called me in to see his latest work. It was on an easel covered with a tattered bedspread. I stood back in anticipation as Freddie unveiled it. On the easel was a four by four-foot canvas thick with paint, and it was all white! There were no subtle tones and no texture. It was solid white! All I could say was, "What do you call it?" I couldn't think of what else to say. "White-on-White," Freddie answered, smiling with pride. That was the last painting he ever did.

Some time later, after leaving the Grove, I heard that Freddy was deeply immersed in the study of arachnids. He was breeding spiders! I often think of Freddy, and the mental picture I have is of him festooned with spider webs.

FRENCHIE IF

If you should ever leave me, go with the dawn before the birds sing their happy songs.

Go gently and quietly with cat-paw steps, so as not to wake me to despair.

JOE COCKER & THE BROWNIES

In the 1960s, there were wild chickens, pigs, and escaped peacocks on the island of Great Exuma. One day when my daughter was four years old, she found a baby chicken in our yard. We adopted it, and within a year it grew into a magnificent rooster. We named him Joe Cocker, and his days were spent outside the kitchen scratching in the leaves under the guava tree where he slept at night.

Each dawn, Joe crowed to the rising sun, and his calls were soon answered by four hens that appeared like magic out of the bush. Soon, crowing, squawking, and pleasure sounds were emanating from the guava tree, and we were finding nests with eggs in the bushes.

Life was good for Joe Cocker, the rooster and his hens. He lived well. There was plenty of food under the tree, and he had a bevy of hens to satisfy his animal lust.

One day while defrosting our deep freezer, I found some marijuana brownies that had been hidden away from the children the year before. I crumbled the brownies and tossed them out the door for Joe and the hens. There was a mad scramble as they converged on the unexpected feast. It took about twenty minutes for the marijuana to take effect, and the result was spectacular! Although it was only mid-day, Joe raised his head to the sky and crowed. Then he took off after the nearest hen, intent on rape. There were squawks of terror, flurries of feathers, and Joe went after another hen. The mayhem continued until late afternoon when Joe and his harem flew into the guava tree, tucked their heads under their wings and fell asleep.

PAIN KILLERS

Drugs weren't a big problem in the 1930s and 40s, except for the people using them. LSD and crack had not come on the scene then. Bahamian police were more concerned with thievery and maintaining old world decency on Bay Street.

In those days, if a female appeared on Bay Street in shorts or a bathing suit, a policeman would politely advise her to change.

Police were recruited from other islands of the West Indie colonies to prevent nepotism. Of course, many of them married local women, had children, and by the 1950s, the police force was all Bahamian.

Marijuana wasn't as popular then as it is today. It was the drug of choice for many musicians, and there were some who chose cocaine or heroin (notably Gene Crupa, the American drummer). One of Sir Harry Oakes' sons was a heroin addict, and it led to his suicide.

One could purchase a bottle of "Pain Killer" in any grocery store in the islands. It came in a plain bottle with no brand name and no medication instructions. Being a tincture of laudanum, it was effective and quite popular for migraine headaches and toothaches. Nowadays, the product does not exist.

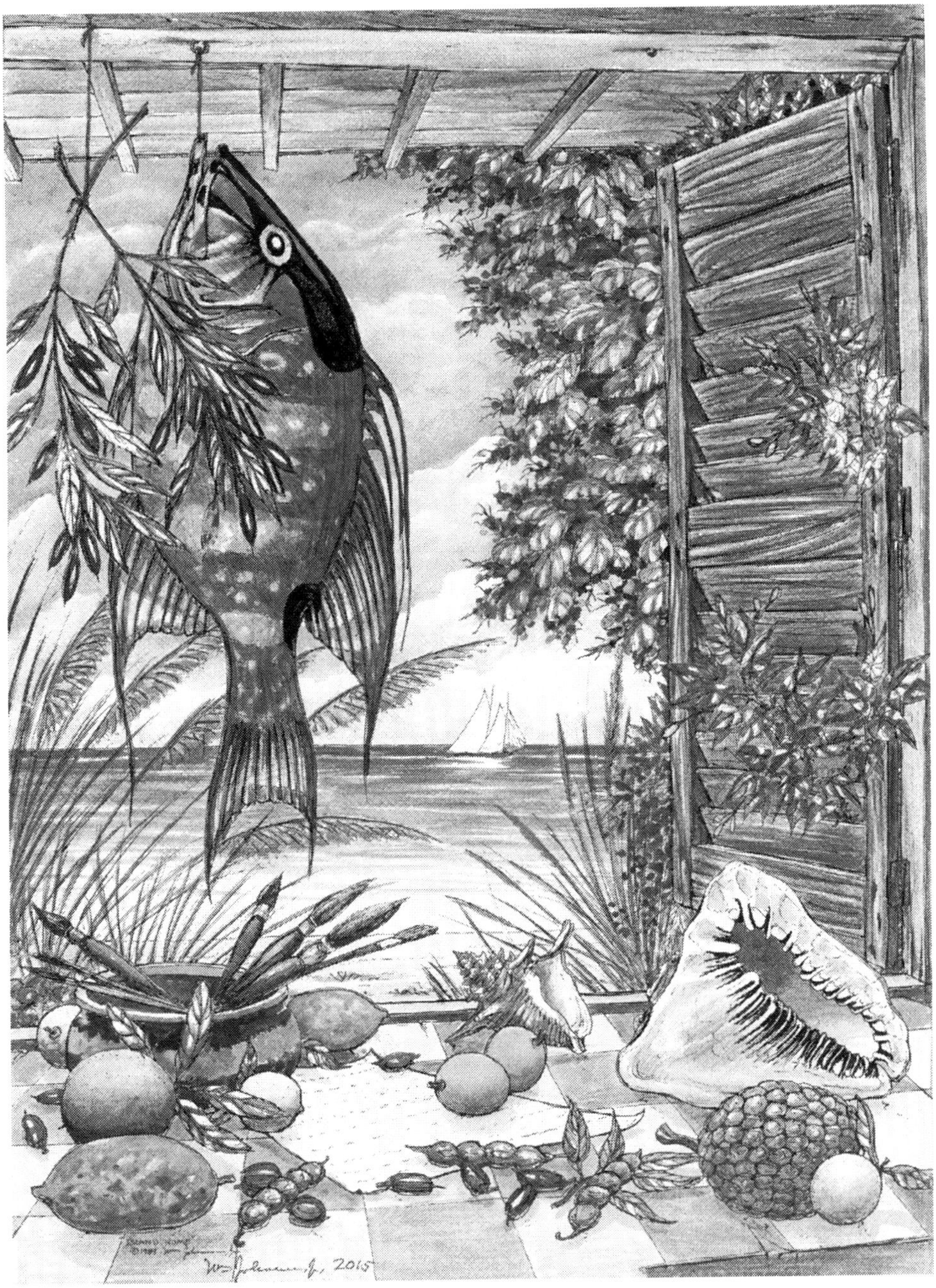
2015

PREGUNTAS

Ask me if I have known blood-red dawns, and I will answer: "The clouds were the colour of her lips."
Ask me if I have seen jungles in the rain, and I will answer: "Her eyes were such a colour."
Ask me how happy I was beside her in the night, and I'll reply: "I was in love!"
But don't ask me where she went that windswept morning.
I have no answer.
Do I miss those lips, those eyes, and her body next to mine?
I answer, "Yes!"

SPRING RAIN

When I was young, spring rain brought dreams of romance. Now there's only lightning and thunder to scare my cat, and whispering rain before the mosquitoes arrive.

If I try hard enough, I can evoke those long-ago feelings on gray days, when the palms are wet and the wind is howling high in the sky.
But the older I get the harder it is to do.

THE LAST COMMANDO

At the start of WWII, a sixteen-year-old British lad lied about his age and joined Lord Lovat's Commandos, then training in Scotland. As a boy of seventeen, he fought his way from Normandy to Belgium and was later transferred to India under Lord Mountbatten.

At the end of the war, he was in charge of captured Japanese soldiers being used as a police force in Southeast Asia. He was a survivor.

Allan had been sailing to Abaco every winter for the past twenty years when I first met him in Hope Town Harbour. He was aboard his sloop "Whisker" with an old Siamese cat he called Mister Mischief. The cat was 15 years old and was as shrivelled and wrinkled as his owner.

Last Christmas (2009) I received a card from Allan in the States, saying Mister Mischief had turned 17 in September and they would be seeing me soon in Abaco. That Christmas card was the last I heard from Allan. I asked about him among my boating friends, but there's been no news.

It's 2013 now and I believe the last Commando is no longer. Allan loved his cat as much as I love my Frenchie. He told me once that they had been together every day but three in all those years.

God bless the last Commando.

THE TIBURON PENINSULA
7.2 Earthquake

On my first trip from Cuba back to the Bahamas, I was blown off course by a storm in the Windward Passage. I ended up in the western Gulf of Gonaive, north of the Tiburon Peninsula. In the pre-dawn light, I saw the blue hills of Haiti in the south. As the sun rose, a shoreline came into view and a glint of silver caught my eye. Having no idea where I was, I set a course for land.

After several hours of tacking towards the glint of light, I saw that it came from the spires of a Gothic cathedral. Bear in mind, that in those days my navigation was quite primitive. All I had aboard Island Girl was a compass, a chronometer, and an antique merchant marine sextant. In those days, there were no satellite or GPS systems, and both the British Admiralty and the United States Hydrographic charts were profoundly inaccurate. For years I had no radio. So, I relied on weather signs and scanned the sky changes. My only excuse for getting lost was that it was my first west to east crossing of the Windward Passage, and I had yet to learn of the diurnal wind-changes there.

By noon, I was anchored off a village of perhaps a hundred souls. A stream flowed through it to the sea where women were doing laundry and children played on the shore. Above all of this loomed a small-scale cast-iron Gothic cathedral. It had been painted with silver metal primer to preserve it from the salt air.

Later, when I researched this, I found that when the French occupied Haiti, they had the cathedral cast in sections in Europe and sent them by ship to Port au Prince, the capitol. The ship foundered at the village of Ti Trou de Nipe, so it was assembled there. It stands there still, with its windows gaping black where stained glass should be. The village fishermen told me they often see coloured glass on the sea bottom, and the children find water-worn pieces on the beach.

After waiting two days for the weather to settle, I weighed anchor, caught the early morning offshore breeze, and set a course for Mole St. Nicholas, and then northward and home to Nassau.

THERE WAS A WOMAN

There was a woman so beautiful that wherever she went the sea was calm.

Even at my age I believe it's possible. My romantic nature cannot be quelled, because I believe in love!

There's nothing more beautiful than a woman awake from sleep with tousled hair and a dream in her eyes. Her image not perfect but with a bit of mystery. Was it Poe who said, "There is some strangeness in all beauty?"

SPLICED BOOM
NATIVE BOAT SKETCHES
EXPLORATIONS LTD. NASSAU
© By WD Johnson, Jr, 2002
CHAINPLATE BRACES
2 MASTHEADS
RUDDER
FORWARD BITTS
GAFF & BOOM JAWS

TRADING SCHOONERS

One usually associates trading schooners with the South Seas where sailboats plied the islands trading for cargos of copra and beche de mer. In the 1920s and 30s, there was a schooner in the Bahamas, reminiscent of those Pacific traders. It was a 60-foot gaff-rigged vessel owned by an elderly couple from Florida. That was before my time. They were my grandfather's friends.

Every Spring, the couple stocked their vessel with a variety of goods; pots and pans, lanterns and tools of all sorts, sail canvas, bolts of cloth, and other items. They sailed yearly to the southern Bahamas, touching at every settlement, where they gave away provisions or traded for fruit, vegetables, fish, and chickens. When asked why they gave away their supplies instead of selling them, the couple said that the islanders were their children and had to be taken care of. It was a valuable service for people who were isolated and cut off from the outside world.

By 1940, the islands were being supplied by regularly scheduled mail boats, the schooner had been lost, destroyed in a hurricane, and the old couple was dead. An era had ended.

WATER SPOUTS

In times past, spongers and smack boat fishermen said that a waterspout was the tail of the devil sitting on the clouds above. To make it go away, they would cut it symbolically with an iron object such as a knife or a cutlass.

This killing of a water spout goes back to the days of the Spanish Main when cannons were fired at threatening waterspouts, and they would miraculously disappear. It was not the cannon ball that destroyed the waterspout. It was the sound waves from the shot.

Today, sailors sound air horns or fire a shotgun to break up waterspouts. In chapter twenty of the novel Moby Dick, Captain Ahab fires a pistol to "kill" a waterspout.

ABOUT THE AUTHOR, WM. JOHNSON

Captain Johnson (William "Bill" Royster Johnson, Jr.) born September 29, 1931, has spent his years sailing the Bahamas, Cuba, and Haiti in his Abaco Ketch 'Island Girl.' He has kept journals and logbooks documenting his experiences with many of the now forever-gone spongers, turtlemen, and fishermen of these islands. He has put his biological training and artistic talents to good use by collecting information on bush medicine and natural history.

Bill may be most well-known for his detailed watercolour maps. Over the years, Bill surveyed and depicted with astonishing accuracy, many of the islands that make up the Bahamas.

Over the years Johnson has garnered sea stories and folklore tales from many sources. From childhood, his heroes have always been the men of these islands that make their livings on the sea.

The art and writings of William "Bill" Johnson attempts to capture and preserve the natural beauty of the Bahamas by depicting Bahamian sea and sky, sail craft, fish, flora, and cultural way of life.

Bill's authentic lifestyle has enabled him to become intimately familiar with his subjects and to paint them against a natural backdrop of sea and sky. People who have studied the Bahamas applaud the accuracy of his work. Special recognition has been given to his prints of Bahamian fishing gear and sailing craft. Bill is also an author of several books including 'Bahama Tales' and 'Bahamian Sailing Craft,' which can be found in the National Watercraft Collection at the Smithsonian Institute in Washington, D.C. and in the National Archives in Nassau, Bahamas.

As Bill enters into his 90's, he embarks on new adventures. Bill spends his days in deep remembrance of a life well travelled, full of richness, exploration, discovery and always a lady nearby. Bill's stories are never met without romance as he explores the catalogs of memory and experience in his mind. It is my honor to help him capture these memories and pour into text, so he can gift to us these captivating and passionate adventures once again as he remembers them.

Rob Waldner

Made in the USA
Columbia, SC
02 October 2024